D1142182

THE NEW TEMPLE SHAKESPEARE

Edited by M. R. Ridley, M.A.

ANTONY AND CLEOPATRA

by William Shakespeare

London: J. M. DENT & SONS LTD.
New York: E. P. DUTTON & CO. INC.

Editor's General Note

The Text. The editor has kept before him the aim of presenting to the modern reader the nearest possible approximation to what Shakespeare actually wrote. The text is therefore conservative, and is based on the earliest reliable printed text. But to avoid distraction (*a*) the spelling is modernised, and (*b*) a limited number of universally accepted emendations is admitted without comment. Where a Quarto text exists as well as the First Folio the passages which occur only in the Quarto are enclosed in square brackets [ ] and those which occur only in the Folio in brace brackets { }.

Scene Division. The rapid continuity of the Elizabethan curtainless production is lost by the 'traditional' scene divisions. Where there is an essential difference of place these scene divisions are retained. Where on the other hand the change of place is insignificant the scene division is indicated only by a space on the page. For ease of reference, however, the 'traditional' division is retained at the head of the page and in line numbering.

Notes. Passages on which there are notes are indicated by a † in the margin.

Punctuation adheres more closely than has been usual to the 'Elizabethan' punctuation of the early texts. It is often therefore more indicative of the way in which the lines were to be delivered than of their syntactical construction.

Glossaries are arranged on a somewhat novel principle, not alphabetically, but in the order in which the words or phrases occur. The editor is much indebted to Mr J. N. Bryson for his collaboration in the preparation of the glossaries.

Preface

The Text. The play was printed for the first time in the First Folio. The text is on the whole good, and apart from a limited number of obvious corruptions the main weakness is a good deal of mislineation.

Date of Composition. A play of the same title, and probably this play, was registered in May 1608. An almost complete consensus of opinion puts its composition in the year 1607-8. Sir Edmund Chambers would put it early in 1607 on the evidence of alterations, apparently based on it, made by Daniel in 1607 in his *Cleopatra* of 1594.

Source. The main, and perhaps the only, source is North's *Plutarch*. The general run of the story, and many of the minor episodes, are taken directly from North; but, with the exception of a few passages (notably the description of Cleopatra's barge and some of Antony's dying words), the direct verbal debt is less than in *Coriolanus*.

Duration of Action. The historic time covered is about twelve years, from 42-30 B.C. The time represented on the stage is probably twelve days, with intervals. The detailed analysis is more complicated than profitable.

Criticism. The play stands apart from the 'four great tragedies.' In the first place, it is a 'love tragedy,' in a sense the *Romeo and Juliet* of a mature man; and that the man who wrote the one play could within twelve or thirteen years write the other shows the bitter rapidity of the maturing. In the second place, we feel in reading it little of that sense of waste which we feel in reading the others. When Antony says 'the nobleness of life is to do thus,' we know that his values in general are wrong, but that for himself, and perhaps too for Cleopatra, he is stating the mere truth. Their passion ennobles them as nothing else ever has or ever could, but also as, if they were in themselves nobler, it would not. And we know, too, that for the world it is better that the course of the Roman state should on, cracking their link asunder. (It is worth noticing how strongly in the first three acts by touch after touch the relentless greatness of Rome is forced upon us, and how helpless before it we feel even Cleopatra, even Antony, to be, or any individual however great.)

Coleridge's estimate of the play is well known. " The highest praise, or rather form of praise, of this play which I can offer in my own mind, is the doubt which its perusal always occasions in me, whether it is not in all exhibitions of a giant power in its strength and vigour of maturity, a formidable rival of the *Macbeth*, *Lear*, *Othello* and *Hamlet*." Even a momentary doubt whether *Antony and Cleopatra* may not be ranked along with the other four is surely just a critical aberration. The play has little dramatic tension, none of that complication followed by explication of plot that marks the others, none of that slowly tightening strain upon the emotions which, particularly in *Othello*, becomes so nearly intolerable. But that is not to say that Shakespeare tried to write a tragedy like *Othello* or *Hamlet* and failed ; he tried to write a drama of a different order, and royally succeeded. The different order may be also an inferior order, but for sheer technical brilliance the play is Shake-speare's high-water mark. In the first place he is handling recalcitrant material. The story of Antony's relations to Cleopatra is not essentially dramatic at all; there is no progress, merely an oscillation. Under various influences—loyalty to Octavia, loyalty to Rome, and, by far the strongest, love of being a great fighting general and leading his adoring troops—Antony swings like a compass needle, but comes to rest always pointing again to the inevitable north. And if this is to be made a great subject, Antony must be given a greatness other than that of his character. We must feel him as a figure whose fate matters to the world; we must ourselves stand under the 'arch of the rang'd empire'; we must not only be told that he is the triple pillar of the world, we must see him so, as the great triumvir, or we care little whether or no he is transformed into a strumpet's fool. And so Shakespeare discards the unities and hurries us about the world, so that we feel the surge of great events and Antony's greatness among them, as determined things hold their way to destiny. And the greater that Antony is made, even in this way, the greater, by an illogical but natural implication, do we feel to be the woman who so enslaves him, and (moving farther round the same circle) the greater she becomes the less do we feel wonder or distress at Antony's subjugation.

As to the style of the play, Coleridge comes nearest to describing it in his two famous phrases, one quoted and one his own, 'feliciter audax' and 'happy valiancy.' The play is full of phrases like *the odds is gone, And there is nothing left remarkable Beneath the visiting moon*, phrases which yield their content only to the reader who runs, and not to the reader who stumbles into them with dictionary and grammar. And it is full, too, of Shakespeare's topmost achievements in 'dramatic' poetry, that poetry which is little remarkable apart from its context, but in its dramatic context indefinably moving. *I am dying, Egypt, dying,* five (or four) very ordinary words and one proper name, as they stand prosaic enough; but in the mouth of the dying Antony, spoken to his royal lover, his serpent of old Nile, they are potent and poignant magic. Even the famous

> *Peace, peace !*
> *Dost thou not see my baby at my breast,*
> *That sucks the nurse asleep ?*

are, out of their setting, little more than lovely lines; but it is Cleopatra the queen who speaks them, robed and crowned for the last of her lovers, and with the asp at her breast. And the effect of some of these passages is yet further heightened by the 'echoes' of which the play is curiously full, a few of which are perhaps worth indicating :

Ant. *Unarm, Eros, the long day's task is done,*
   And we must sleep. (IV. xiv. 35.)

Iras. *Finish, good lady, the bright day is done,*
   And we are for the dark. (V. ii. 193.)

Ant.   *I will be*
   A bridegroom in my death, and run into't
   As to a lover's bed. (IV. xiv. 99.)

Cleo. *The stroke of death is as a lover's pinch,*
   Which hurts, and is desir'd. (V. ii. 295.)

x

> Cleo. *When thou hast done this chare I'll give thee leave*
> *To play till doomsday.* (V. ii. 231.)

> Char. *Your crown's awry;*
> *I'll mend it, and then play.* (V. ii. 318.)

And, of a rather different order and less importance, such things as the two views of Cleopatra as Cæsar's 'morsel':

> Cleo. *Broad-fronted Cæsar,*
> *When thou wast here above the ground, I was*
> *A morsel for a monarch.* (I. v. 29.)

> Ant. *I found you as a morsel, cold upon*
> *Dead Cæsar's trencher.* (III. xiii. 116.)

or Enobarbus' echo of Antony's comment on his marriage (II. iii. 38 and II. vi. 126), or the two hand-kissings (III. xiii. 123-26 and IV. viii. 23) or Antony's *Thrice nobler than myself* and Cleopatra's *This proves me base* (IV. xiv. 95 and V. ii. 300), or the chime on the word *royal* in the last scene (318, 327, 335).

On the two main characters opinions have differed widely. Here are a few on Antony:—" Antony is dissolute and voluptuous, and Cleopatra's depravity is congenial to his nature." " A man of the most noble and high spirit, capable at times of a thoroughly soldier-like life and full of kind and generous feelings." " The passion of Antony for Cleopatra is too obviously spurious to command our sympathy." (!) " Antony appears as the soldier and the voluptuary, swayed alternately by love, by regret, by ambition, at one moment the great ruler of the divided world, at the next flinging his future away at the dictation of a passionate caprice."

ANTONY AND CLEOPATRA

Cleopatra gravels the critics of later ages as completely as she did those of her own. She is " a brilliant antithesis," " a compound of contradictions " or (perhaps the best example of this meaningless verbiage of befuddled bewilderment) " this glorious riddle, whose dazzling complexity continually mocks and eludes us." She is often described as a " courtesan of genius," but that phrase in isolation is fair neither to Cleopatra nor to the penetrating criticism from which it is isolated. " Cleopatra is the greatest of the enchantresses. She has wit, grace, humour; the intoxication of sex breathes from her; she unites the passion of a great temperament with the fathomless coquetry of a courtesan of genius. . . . It is this magnificence which invests Cleopatra's criminality with a kind of sublimity, so vast is the scale of her being, and so tremendous the force of her passions." Perhaps, after all, the best description of her is Enobarbus' simple ' a wonderful piece of work.' That at least avoids any of those idle questionings as to the morality or immorality of the love of Antony and Cleopatra in which one school of critics gets itself so sadly entangled.

I propose to quote *in extenso* only two pieces of criticism, both from Professor A. C. Bradley's lecture on the play in his *Oxford Lectures on Poetry*, partly because that lecture (like the one in the same book on *The Rejection of Falstaff*) is perhaps less well known than it should be, being unduly overshadowed by *Shakespearian Tragedy*, but more because it seems to me to say all that needs to be said as well as it is possible to say it. And it is an interesting comment on the quality of the play and of its heroine that they can inspire this great but commonly austere critic to the slow crescendo and superb climax of the second extract, surely (in spite of an odd geographical lapse) as splendid a piece of imaginative indeed poetic, criticism as has ever been written in English.

" The first of living soldiers, an able politician, a most persuasive orator, Antony nevertheless was not born to rule the world. He enjoys being a great man, but he has not the love of rule for rule's sake. Power for him is chiefly a means to pleasure. The pleasure he wants is so huge that he needs a huge power; but half the world, even a third of it, would suffice. . . . A man who loved power as much as thousands of insignificant people love it would have made a sterner struggle than Antony's against his enchantment. He can hardly be said to struggle at all. He brings himself to leave Cleopatra only because he knows he will return. In every moment of his absence, whether the wake or sleep, a siren music in his blood is singing him back to her; and to this music, however he may be occupied, the soul within him leans and listens. The joy of life had always culminated for him in the love of women: he could say ' no ' to none of them: of Octavia herself he speaks like a poet. When he meets Cleopatra he finds his Absolute. She satisfies, nay glorifies, his whole being. She intoxicates his senses. Her wiles, her taunts, her furies and meltings, her laughter and tears, bewitch him all alike. She loves what he loves, and she surpasses him. She can drink him to his bed, out-jest his practical jokes, out-act the best actress who ever amused him, out-dazzle his own magnificence. She is his playfellow, and yet a great queen. Angling in the river, playing billiards, flourishing the sword he used at Philippi, hopping forty paces in a public street, she remains an enchantress. Her spirit is made of wind and flame, and the poet in him worships her no less than the man. He is under no illusion about her, knows all her faults, sees through her wiles, believes her capable of betraying him. It makes no difference. She is his heart's desire made perfect. To love her is what he was born for. What have the gods in heaven to say against it? To imagine heaven is to imagine her; to die is to rejoin her. To deny that this is love is the madness of morality. He gives her every atom of his heart."

.   .   .   .   .   .

"It seems to us perfectly natural, nay, in a sense perfectly right, that her lover should be her slave; that her women should adore her and die with her; that Enobarbus, who foresaw what must happen, and who opposes her wishes and braves her anger, should talk of her with rapture and feel no bitterness against her; that Dolabella, after a minute's conversation, should betray to her his master's intention and enable her to frustrate it. And when Octavius shows himself proof against her fascination, instead of admiring him we turn from him with disgust and think him a disgrace to his species. Why? It is not that we consider him bound to fall in love with her. Enobarbus did not; Dolabella did not; we ourselves do not. The feeling she inspires was felt then, and is felt now, by women no less than men, and would have been shared by Octavia herself. Doubtless she wrought magic on the senses, but she had not extraordinary beauty, like Helen's, such beauty as seems divine. Plutarch says so. The man who wrote the sonnets to the dark lady would have known it for himself. He goes out of his way to add to her age, and tells us of her wrinkles and the waning of her lip. But Enobarbus, in his very mockery, calls her a wonderful piece of work. Dolabella interrupts her with the cry, 'Most sovereign creature,' and we echo it. . . . That which makes her wonderful and sovereign laughs at definition, but she herself came nearest naming it when, in the final speech (a passage surpassed in poetry, if at all, only by the final speech of Othello), she cries:

I am fire and air ; my other elements
I give to baser life.

The fire and air which at death break from union with those other elements, transfigured them during her life, and still convert into engines of enchantment the very things for which she is condemned. I can refer only to one. She loves Antony. We should marvel at her less and love her more if she loved him more—loved him well enough to follow him at once to death; but it is to blunder strangely to doubt that she loved him, or that her glorious description of him (though it was also meant to work on Dolabella) came from her heart. Only the spirit of fire and air within her refuses to be trammelled or extinguished; burns its way through the obstacles of fortune and even through the resistance of her love and grief; and would lead her undaunted to fresh life and the conquest of new worlds. It is this which makes her ' strong toil of grace ' unbreakable; speaks in her brows' bent and every tone and movement; glorifies the arts and the rages which in another would merely disgust or amuse us; and, in the final scenes of her life, flames into such brilliance that we watch her entranced as she struggles for freedom, and thrilled with triumph as, conquered, she puts her conqueror to scorn and goes to meet her lover in the splendour that crowned and robed her long ago, when her barge burnt on the water like a burnished throne, and she floated to Cydnus on the enamoured stream to take him captive for ever." [1]

[1] This passage is reprinted by permission of the Publishers, Messrs Macmillan & Co.

ANTONY AND CLEOPATRA

DRAMATIS PERSONÆ

ANTONY,
OCTAVIUS CÆSAR, } *triumvirs.*
LEPIDUS,
SEXTUS POMPEIUS.

DOMITIUS ENOBARBUS,
VENTIDIUS,
EROS,
SCARUS,
DERCETAS, } *friends to Antony.*
DEMETRIUS,
PHILO,

MÆCENAS,
AGRIPPA,
DOLABELLA,
PROCULEIUS, } *friends to Cæsar.*
THYREUS,
GALLUS,

MENAS,
MENECRATES, } *friends to Sextus Pompeius.*
VARRIUS,

TAURUS, *lieutenant-general to Cæsar.*
CANIDIUS, *lieutenant-general to Antony.*
SILIUS, *an officer in Ventidius's army.*
EUPHRONIUS, *a schoolmaster.*
ALEXAS,
MARDIAN, *a eunuch,* } *attendants on Cleopatra.*
SELEUCUS,
DIOMEDES,
LAMPRIUS, *a soothsayer.*   A Clown.

CLEOPATRA, *queen of Egypt.*
OCTAVIA, *sister to Cæsar, and wife to Antony.*
CHARMIAN, } *attendants on Cleopatra.*
IRAS,

Officers, Soldiers, Messengers, and other Attendants.

SCENE: *In several parts of the Roman Empire.*

ANTONY AND CLEOPATRA

Act First

SCENES I, II, AND III

Alexandria.   Cleopatra's palace

Enter Demetrius and Philo

Phi. Nay, but this dotage of our general's
O'erflows the measure : those his goodly eyes,
That o'er the files and musters of the war
Have glow'd like plated Mars, now bend, now turn
The office and devotion of their view
Upon a tawny front.   His captain's heart,
Which in the scuffles of great fights hath burst
The buckles on his breast, reneges all temper,
And is become the bellows and the fan
To cool a gipsy's lust.

                  Look where they come :   10
Take but good note, and you shall see in him
The triple pillar of the world transform'd
Into a strumpet's fool.   Behold and see.

*Flourish.   Enter Antony, Cleopatra, her Ladies, the train,
with Eunuchs fanning her*

Cle. If it be love indeed, tell me how much.

1

Ant. There 's beggary in the love that can be reckon'd.

Cle. I 'll set a bourn how far to be belov'd.

Ant. Then must thou needs find out new heaven, new earth.

Enter a Messenger

Mes. News, my good lord, from Rome.

Ant.   Grates me, the sum.

Cle. Nay, hear them, Antony :

Fulvia perchance is angry ; or who knows   20

If the scarce-bearded Cæsar have not sent

His powerful mandate to you, ' Do this, or this ;

Take in that kingdom, and enfranchise that ;

Perform 't, or else we damn thee.'

Ant.   How, my love ?

Cle. Perchance ? nay, and most like :

You must not stay here longer, your dismission

Is come from Cæsar, therefore hear it, Antony.

Where 's Fulvia's process ?   (Cæsar 's I would say.)

     Both ?

Call in the messengers.   As I am Egypt's queen,

Thou blushest, Antony, and that blood of thine   30

Is Cæsar's homager : else so thy cheek pays shame

When shrill-tongu'd Fulvia scolds.   The messengers !

Ant. Let Rome in Tiber melt, and the wide arch

Of the rang'd empire fall !   Here is my space ;

Kingdoms are clay : our dungy earth alike

Feeds beast as man ; the nobleness of life
Is to do thus : when such a mutual pair   *Embracing*
And such a twain can do 't, in which I bind,
On pain of punishment, the world to weet
We stand up peerless.

Cle.   Excellent falsehood !   40
Why did he marry Fulvia, and not love her ?
I 'll seem the fool I am not ; Antony
Will be himself.

Ant.   But stirr'd by Cleopatra.
Now for the love of Love, and her soft hours,
Let 's not confound the time with conference harsh :
There 's not a minute of our lives should stretch
Without some pleasure now.   What sport to-night ?

Cle. Hear the ambassadors.

Ant.   Fie, wrangling queen ;
Whom every thing becomes, to chide, to laugh,
To weep ; whose every passion fully strives   50
To make itself, in thee, fair, and admir'd !
No messenger but thine, and all alone
To-night we 'll wander through the streets, and note
The qualities of people.   Come, my queen,
Last night you did desire it.   Speak not to us.

                    Exeunt Antony and Cleopatra with their train

*Dem.*Is Cæsar with Antonius priz'd so slight ?

Phi. Sir, sometimes, when he is not Antony,
  He comes too short of that great property
  Which still should go with Antony.
Dem.   I am full sorry
  That he approves the common liar, who   60
  Thus speaks of him at Rome ; but I will hope
  Of better deeds to-morrow. Rest you happy !

               Exeunt

Enter Enobarbus, Lamprius a Soothsayer, Rannius, Lucilius, †
  Charmian, Iras, Mardian, and Alexas

Cha. Lord Alexas, sweet Alexas, most any thing Alexas,
  almost most absolute Alexas, where 's the soothsayer
  that you prais'd so to the queen ? O, that I knew
  this husband, which, you say, must change his horns †
  with garlands !
Al. Soothsayer !
Lam. Your will ?
Cha. Is this the man ? Is 't you, sir, that know things ?
Lam. In nature's infinite book of secrecy
  A little I can read.

Al.   Show him your hand.   10

Eno. Bring in the banquet quickly ; wine enough
     Cleopatra's health to drink.

Cha. Good sir, give me good fortune.

Lam. I make not, but foresee.

Cha. Pray then, foresee me one.

Lam. You shall be yet far fairer than you are.

Cha. He means in flesh.

Iras. No, you shall paint when you are old.

Cha. Wrinkles forbid !

Al. Vex not his prescience, be attentive.   20

Cha. Hush !

Lam. You shall be more beloving than belov'd.

Cha. I had rather heat my liver with drinking.

Al. Nay, hear him.

Cha. Good now, some excellent fortune ! Let me be
     married to three kings in a forenoon, and widow them
     all : let me have a child at fifty, to whom Herod †
     of Jewry may do homage : find me to marry me
     with Octavius Cæsar, and companion me with my
     mistress.   30

Lam. You shall outlive the lady whom you serve.

Cha. O excellent !   I love long life better than figs. †

Lam. You have seen and prov'd a fairer former fortune
     Than that which is to approach.

Cha. Then belike my children shall have no names:
    prithee, how many boys and wenches must I have?

Lam. If every of your wishes had a womb,
    And fertile every wish, a million.

Cha. Out, fool! I forgive thee for a witch.

Al. You think none but your sheets are privy to your   40
    wishes.

Cha. Nay, come, tell Iras hers.

Al. We 'll know all our fortunes.

Eno. Mine, and most of our fortunes to-night, shall be,
    drunk to bed.

Iras. There 's a palm presages chastity, if nothing else.

Cha. E'en as the o'erflowing Nilus presageth famine.

Iras. Go, you wild bedfellow, you cannot soothsay.

Cha. Nay, if an oily palm be not a fruitful prognostication,
    I cannot scratch mine ear. Prithee, tell her but a   50
    worky-day fortune.

Lam. Your fortunes are alike—

Iras. But how, but how? give me particulars.

Lam. I have said.

Iras. Am I not an inch of fortune better than she?

Cha. Well, if you were but an inch of fortune better
    than I, where would you choose it?

Iras. Not in my husband's nose.

Cha. Our worser thoughts heavens mend! Alexas,—

come, his fortune, his fortune !   O, let him marry a   60
woman that cannot go, sweet Isis, I beseech thee,
and let her die too, and give him a worse, and let
worse follow worse, till the worst of all follow
him laughing to his grave, fifty-fold a cuckold !
Good Isis, hear me this prayer, though thou deny
me a matter of more weight ;   good Isis, I beseech
thee !

Iras. Amen, dear goddess, hear that prayer of the people !
for, as it is a heart-breaking to see a handsome
man loose-wiv'd, so it is a deadly sorrow to behold   70
a foul knave uncuckolded : therefore, dear Isis,
keep decorum, and fortune him accordingly !

Cha. Amen.

Al. Lo, now, if it lay in their hands to make me a
cuckold, they would make themselves whores, but
they 'ld do 't !

Eno. Hush ! here comes Antony.

Cha.   Not he, the queen.

Enter Cleopatra

Cle. Saw you my lord ?

Eno. No, lady.

Cle. Was he not here ?   80

Cha. No, madam.

Cle. He was dispos'd to mirth, but on the sudden

    A Roman thought hath struck him.   Enobarbus !

Eno. Madam ?

Cle. Seek him, and bring him hither.   Where 's Alexas ?

Al. Here at your service.   My lord approaches.

Cle. We will not look upon him : go with us.   *Exeunt*
        Enter Antony with a Messenger and Attendants

Mes. Fulvia thy wife first came into the field.

Ant. Against my brother Lucius ?

Mes. Ay :   90

    But soon that war had end, and the time's state
    Made friends of them, jointing their force 'gainst
        Cæsar,
    Whose better issue in the war from Italy
    Upon the first encounter drave them.

Ant.   Well, what worst ?

Mes. The nature of bad news infects the teller.

Ant. When it concerns the fool or coward.   On :
    Things that are past are done, with me.   'Tis thus ;
    Who tells me true, though in his tale lie death,
    I hear him as he flatter'd.

Mes.   Labienus

    (This is stiff news) hath with his Parthian force   100
    Extended Asia : from Euphrates   †
    His conquering banner shook, from Syria
    To Lydia and to Ionia,

Whilst—

Ant.   Antony, thou wouldst say,—

Mes.   O, my lord !

Ant. Speak to me home, mince not the general tongue,
　　　Name Cleopatra as she is call'd in Rome ;
　　　Rail thou in Fulvia's phrase, and taunt my faults
　　　With such full license, as both truth and malice
　　　Have power to utter.   O, then we bring forth
　　　　　weeds   110
　　　When our quick minds lie still, and our ills told us
　　　Is as our earing.   Fare thee well awhile.

Mes. At your noble pleasure.   *Exit*

Ant. From Sicyon, ho, the news !   Speak there !

1.A. The man from Sicyon, is there such an one ?

2.A. He stays upon your will.

Ant.   Let him appear.
　　　These strong Egyptian fetters I must break,
　　　Or lose myself in dotage.

　　　　　　　Enter another Messenger
　　　　　　　　What are you ?

2.M. Fulvia thy wife is dead.

Ant.   Where died she ?

2.M. In Sicyon :   120
　　　Her length of sickness, with what else more serious
　　　Importeth thee to know, this bears.   *Gives a letter*

9

Ant.   Forbear me.

Exit Sec. Messenger

There's a great spirit gone!   Thus did I desire it:
What our contempts doth often hurl from us,
We wish it ours again; the present pleasure,
By revolution lowering, does become
The opposite of itself: she's good, being gone;
The hand could pluck her back that shov'd her on.
I must from this enchanting queen break off,
Ten thousand harms, more than the ills I know,   130
My idleness doth hatch.   How now!   Enobarbus!

Re-enter Enobarbus

Eno. What's your pleasure, sir?

Ant. I must with haste from hence.

Eno. Why then we kill all our women.   We see how
mortal an unkindness is to them; if they suffer
our departure, death's the word.

Ant. I must be gone.

Eno. Under a compelling occasion, let women die: it
were pity to cast them away for nothing, though,
between them and a great cause, they should be   140
esteemed nothing.   Cleopatra, catching but the
least noise of this, dies instantly; I have seen her
die twenty times upon far poorer moment: I do

think there is mettle in death, which commits some
loving act upon her, she hath such a celerity in
dying.

Ant. She is cunning past man's thought.

Eno. Alack, sir, no, her passions are made of nothing but
the finest part of pure love : we cannot call her
winds and waters sighs and tears ; they are greater 150
storms and tempests than almanacs can report :
this cannot be cunning in her ; if it be, she makes
a shower of rain as well as Jove.

Ant. Would I had never seen her !

Eno. O, sir, you had then left unseen a wonderful piece
of work, which not to have been blest withal would
have discredited your travel.

Ant. Fulvia is dead.

Eno. Sir ?

Ant. Fulvia is dead. 160

Eno. Fulvia ?

Ant. Dead.

Eno. Why, sir, give the gods a thankful sacrifice. When
it pleaseth their deities to take the wife of a man
from him, it shows to man the tailors of the earth,
comforting therein, that when old robes are worn
out, there are members to make new. If there were
no more women but Fulvia, then had you indeed

a cut, and the case to be lamented : this grief is
crown'd with consolation ; your old smock brings 170
forth a new petticoat, and indeed the tears live in
an onion that should water this sorrow.

Ant. The business she hath broached in the state
Cannot endure my absence.

Eno. And the business you have broach'd here cannot
be without you, especially that of Cleopatra's, which
wholly depends on your abode.

Ant. No more light answers.   Let our officers
Have notice what we purpose.   I shall break
The cause of our expedience to the queen,   180
And get her leave to part.   For not alone
The death of Fulvia, with more urgent touches,
Do strongly speak to us, but the letters too
Of many our contriving friends in Rome
Petition us at home : Sextus Pompeius
Hath given the dare to Cæsar, and commands
The empire of the sea : our slippery people,
Whose love is never link'd to the deserver,
Till his deserts are past, begin to throw
Pompey the Great, and all his dignities,   190
Upon his son, who, high in name and power,
Higher than both in blood and life, stands up
For the main soldier : whose quality, going on,

The sides o' the world may danger. Much is
    breeding,
Which, like the courser's hair, hath yet but life,   †
And not a serpent's poison. Say our pleasure,
To such whose places under us require,
Our quick remove from hence.

Eno. I shall do 't.

                                     Exeunt

Enter Cleopatra, Charmian, Iras, and Alexas

Cle. Where is he ?

Cha.   I did not see him since.

Cle. See where he is, who' s with him, what he does :
    I did not send you : if you find him sad,
    Say I am dancing ; if in mirth, report
    That I am sudden sick : quick, and return

                               Exit Alexas

Cha. Madam, methinks, if you did love him dearly,
    You do not hold the method to enforce
    The like from him.

Cle.   What should I do, I do not ?

Cha. In each thing give him way, cross him in nothing.

Cle. Thou teachest like a fool : the way to lose him.   10

Cha. Tempt him not so too far ; I wish, forbear,
  In time we hate that which we often fear.
  But here comes Antony.

Enter Antony

Cle.   I am sick, and sullen.

Ant. I am sorry to give breathing to my purpose,—

Cle. Help me away, dear Charmian, I shall fall,
  It cannot be thus long, the sides of nature
  Will not sustain it.

Ant.   Now, my dearest queen,—

Cle. Pray you, stand farther from me.

Ant.   What 's the matter ?

Cle. I know, by that same eye, there 's some good news.
  What says the married woman ; you may go ?   20
  Would she had never given you leave to come !
  Let her not say 'tis I that keep you here,
  I have no power upon you ; hers you are.

Ant. The gods best know—

Cle.   O, never was there queen
  So mightily betray'd ! yet at the first
  I saw the treasons planted.

Ant.   Cleopatra,—

Cle. Why should I think you can be mine, and true,
  (Though you in swearing shake the throned gods)
  Who have been false to Fulvia ?   Riotous madness,

14

To be entangled with those mouth-made vows, 30
Which break themselves in swearing !

Ant.   Most sweet queen—

Cle. Nay, pray you, seek no colour for your going,
But bid farewell, and go : when you sued staying,
Then was the time for words : no going then ;
Eternity was in our lips, and eyes,
Bliss in our brows' bent ; none our parts so poor
But was a race of heaven : they are so still, †
Or thou, the greatest soldier of the world,
Art turn'd the greatest liar.

Ant.   How, now, lady ?

Cle. I would I had thy inches ; thou shouldst know 40
There were a heart in Egypt.

Ant.   Hear me, queen :
The strong necessity of time commands
Our services awhile ; but my full heart
Remains in use with you.   Our Italy
Shines o'er with civil swords : Sextus Pompeius
Makes his approaches to the port of Rome :
Equality of two domestic powers
Breed scrupulous faction : the hated, grown to
        strength,
Are newly grown to love : the condemn'd **Pompey**,
Rich in his father's honour, creeps apace 50

Into the hearts of such as have not thriv'd
Upon the present state, whose numbers threaten,
And quietness, grown sick of rest, would purge
By any desperate change.   My more particular,
And that which most with you should safe my going,
Is Fulvia's death.

Cle. Though age from folly could not give me freedom,
It does from childishness : can Fulvia die ?

Ant. She 's dead, my queen :
Look here, and at thy sovereign leisure read   60
The garboils she awak'd : at the last, best,
See when and where she died.

Cle.   O most false love !
Where be the sacred vials thou shouldst fill
With sorrowful water ?   Now I see, I see,
In Fulvia's death, how mine receiv'd shall be.

Ant. Quarrel no more, but be prepar'd to know
The purposes I bear ; which are, or cease,
As you shall give the advice.   By the fire
That quickens Nilus' slime, I go from hence
Thy soldier, servant, making peace or war   70
As thou affect'st.

Cle.   Cut my lace, Charmian, come,
But let it be, I am quickly ill, and well,
So Antony loves.

16

Ant.   My precious queen, forbear,
          And give true evidence to his love, which stands
          An honourable trial.

Cle.   So Fulvia told me.
          I prithee, turn aside, and weep for me,
          Then bid adieu to me, and say the tears
          Belong to Egypt : good now, play one scene
          Of excellent dissembling, and let it look
          Like perfect honour.

Ant.   You 'll heat my blood, no more.   80

Cle. You can do better yet ; but this is meetly.

Ant. Now, by my sword,—

Cle.   And target.   Still he mends,
          But this is not the best.   Look, prithee, Charmian,
          How this Herculean Roman does become
          The carriage of his chafe.

Ant. I 'll leave you, lady.

Cle.   Courteous lord, one word.
          Sir, you and I must part, but that 's not it :
          Sir, you and I have lov'd, but there 's not it :
          That you know well, something it is I would,—
          O, my oblivion is a very Antony,   90
          And I am all forgotten.

Ant.   But that your royalty
          Holds idleness your subject, I should take you

For idleness itself.

Cle.   'Tis sweating labour
To bear such idleness so near the heart
As Cleopatra this. But, sir, forgive me,
Since my becomings kill me, when they do not
Eye well to you. Your honour calls you hence,
Therefore be deaf to my unpitied folly,
And all the gods go with you ! Upon your sword
Sit laurel victory, and smooth success   100
Be strew'd before your feet !

Ant.   Let us go. Come ;
Our separation so abides and flies,
That thou, residing here, go'st yet with me ;
And I, hence fleeting, here remain with thee.
Away !   *Exeunt*

SCENE IV

Rome. Cæsar's house

*Enter Octavius Cæsar, reading a letter, Lepidus,
and their train*

Cæs. You may see, Lepidus, and henceforth know,
It is not Cæsar's natural vice to hate
Our great competitor : from Alexandria

18

This is the news : he fishes, drinks, and wastes
The lamps of night in revel : is not more manlike
Than Cleopatra ; nor the queen of Ptolemy
More womanly than he : hardly gave audience, or
Vouchsaf'd to think he had partners : you shall find
    there
A man who is the abstract of all faults
That all men follow.

Lep.   I must not think there are   10
Evils enow to darken all his goodness :
His faults in him seem as the spots of heaven,
More fiery by night's blackness ; hereditary
Rather than purchas'd ; what he cannot change
Than what he chooses.

Cæs. You are too indulgent.   Let us grant it is not
Amiss to tumble on the bed of Ptolemy,
To give a kingdom for a mirth, to sit
And keep the turn of tippling with a slave,
To reel the streets at noon, and stand the buffet   20
With knaves that smell of sweat : say this becomes
    him—
(As his composure must be rare indeed
Whom these things cannot blemish) yet must Antony
No way excuse his soils, when we do bear
So great weight in his lightness.   If he fill'd

His vacancy with his voluptuousness,
Full surfeits, and the dryness of his bones,
Call on him for 't : but to confound such time,
That drums him from his sport, and speaks as loud
As his own state, and ours, 'tis to be chid ;   30
As we rate boys, who, being mature in knowledge,
Pawn their experience to their present pleasure,
And so rebel to judgement.

Lep.   Here 's more news.

Enter a Messenger

Mes. Thy biddings have been done, and every hour,
Most noble Cæsar, shalt thou have report
How 'tis abroad.   Pompey is strong at sea,
And it appears he is belov'd of those
That only have fear'd Cæsar : to the ports
The discontents repair, and men's reports
Give him much wrong'd.

Cæs.   I should have known no less :   40
It had been taught us from the primal state,
That he which is was wish'd until he were ;
And the ebb'd man, ne'er lov'd till ne'er worth love,
Comes dear'd by being lack'd.   This common body,
Like to a vagabond flag upon the stream,
Goes to and back, lackeying the varying tide,
To rot itself with motion.

Mes.   Cæsar, I bring thee word,
    Menecrates and Menas, famous pirates,
    Make the sea serve them, which they ear and wound
    With keels of every kind ; many hot inroads   50
    They make in Italy ; the borders maritime
    Lack blood to think on 't, and flush youth revolt :
    No vessel can peep forth, but 'tis as soon
    Taken as seen ; for Pompey's name strikes more
    Than could his war resisted.

Cæs.   Antony,
    Leave thy lascivious wassails.   When thou once
    Wast beaten from Modena, where thou slew'st
    Hirtius and Pansa, consuls, at thy heel
    Did famine follow, whom thou fought'st against,
    (Though daintily brought up) with patience more   60
    Than savages could suffer.   Thou didst drink
    The stale of horses, and the gilded puddle
    Which beasts would cough at : thy palate then did deign
    The roughest berry, on the rudest hedge ;
    Yea, like the stag, when snow the pasture sheets,
    The barks of trees thou browsedst.   On the Alps
    It is reported thou didst eat strange flesh,
    Which some did die to look on : and all this
    (It wounds thine honour that I speak it now)
    Was borne so like a soldier that thy cheek   70

So much as lank'd not.

Lep.   'Tis pity of him.

Cæs. Let his shames quickly
    Drive him to Rome ; 'tis time we twain
    Did show ourselves i' in the field, and to that end
    Assemble we immediate council : Pompey
    Thrives in our idleness.

Lep.   To-morrow, Cæsar,
    I shall be furnish'd to inform you rightly
    Both what by sea and land I can be able   †
    To front this present time.

Cæs.   Till which encounter,
    It is my business too.   Farewell.   80

Lep. Farewell, my lord ; what you shall know meantime
    Of stirs abroad, I shall beseech you, sir,
    To let me be partaker.

Cæs.   Doubt not, sir,
    I know it for my bond.   *Exeunt*

SCENE V

Alexandria.   *Cleopatra's palace*

Enter Cleopatra, Charmian, Iras, and Mardian

Cle. Charmian !

Cha. Madam ?

22

Cle. Ha, ha !
Give me to drink mandragora.

Cha.   Why, madam ?

Cle. That I might sleep out this great gap of time :
My Antony is away.

Cha.   You think of him too much.

Cle. O, 'tis treason !

Cha.   Madam, I trust, not so.

Cle. Thou, eunuch Mardian !

Mar.   What 's your highness' pleasure ?

Cle. Not now to hear thee sing ; I take no pleasure
In aught an eunuch has : 'tis well for thee,   10
That, being unseminar'd, thy freer thoughts
May not fly forth of Egypt.   Hast thou affections ?

Mar. Yes, gracious madam.

Cle. Indeed ?

Mar. Not in deed, madam, for I can do nothing
But what indeed is honest to be done :
Yet have I fierce affections, and think
What Venus did with Mars.

Cle.   O Charmian,
Where think'st thou he is now ?   Stands he, or sits
he ?
Or does he walk ? or is he on his horse ?   20
O happy horse, to bear the weight of Antony !

Do bravely, horse! for wot'st thou whom thou
  mov'st?
The demi-Atlas of this earth, the arm
And burgonet of men. He 's speaking now,
Or murmuring, ' Where 's my serpent of old Nile? '
(For so he calls me :) now I feed myself
With most delicious poison. Think on me,
That am with Phœbus' amorous pinches black
And wrinkled deep in time. Broad-fronted Cæsar,
When thou wast here above the ground, I was 30
A morsel for a monarch : and great Pompey
Would stand and make his eyes grow in my brow,
There would he anchor his aspect, and die
With looking on his life.

      Enter Alexas

Al.   Sovereign of Egypt, hail!
Cle. How much unlike art thou Mark Antony!
 Yet, coming from him, that great medicine hath
 With his tinct gilded thee. How goes it with
 My brave Mark Antony?
Al.   Last thing he did, dear queen,
 He kiss'd—the last of many doubled kisses—
 This orient pearl. His speech sticks in my heart. 40
Cle. Mine ear must pluck it thence.
Al.   ' Good friend,' quoth he,

' Say, the firm Roman to great Egypt sends
This treasure of an oyster ; at whose foot,
To mend the petty present, I will piece
Her opulent throne with kingdoms ; all the east,
(Say thou) shall call her mistress.'   So he nodded,
And soberly did mount an arm-gaunt steed,   †
Who neigh'd so high, that what I would have spoke
Was beastly dumb'd by him.

Cle.   What, was he sad, or merry ?

Al. Like to the time o' the year between the extremes   50
Of hot and cold, he was nor sad nor merry.

Cle. O well divided disposition !   Note him,
Note him, good Charmian, 'tis the man ; but note him :
He was not sad, for he would shine on those
That make their looks by his ; he was not merry,
Which seem'd to tell them his remembrance lay
In Egypt with his joy ; but between both.
O heavenly mingle !   Be'st thou sad, or merry,
The violence of either thee becomes,
So does it no man else.   Met'st thou my posts ?   60

Al. Ay, madam, twenty several messengers :
Why do you send so thick ?

Cle.   Who 's born that day
When I forget to send to Antony,
Shall die a beggar.   Ink and paper, Charmian.

    Welcome, my good Alexas.   Did I, Charmian,
    Ever love Cæsar so ?

Cha.   O that brave Cæsar !

Cle. Be chok'd with such another emphasis !
    Say, the brave Antony.

Cha.   The valiant Cæsar !

Cle. By Isis, I will give thee bloody teeth,
    If thou with Cæsar paragon again   70
    My man of men.

Cha.   By your most gracious pardon,
    I sing but after you.

Cle.   My salad days,
    When I was green in judgement, cold in blood,
    To say as I said then !   But come, away,
    Get me ink and paper ; he shall have every day
    A several greeting, or I 'll unpeople Egypt. *Exeunt*

Act Second

Messina.   Pompey's house

Enter Pompey, Menecrates, and Menas, in warlike manner

Pom. If the great gods be just, they shall assist
    The deeds of justest men.

Menec.   Know, worthy Pompey,
    That what they do delay, they not deny.

Pom. Whiles we are suitors to their throne, decays
    The thing we sue for.

Menec.   We, ignorant of ourselves,
    Beg often our own harms, which the wise powers
    Deny us for our good ; so find we profit
    By losing of our prayers.

Pom.   I shall do well :
    The people love me, and the sea is mine ;
    My powers are crescent, and my auguring hope   10
    Says it will come to the full.   Mark Antony
    In Egypt sits at dinner, and will make
    No wars without doors : Cæsar gets money where
    He loses hearts : Lepidus flatters both,

  Of both is flatter'd ; but he neither loves,
  Nor either cares for him.

Menas.   Cæsar and Lepidus
  Are in the field, a mighty strength they carry.

Pom. Where have you this ? 'tis false.

Menas.   From Silvius, sir.

Pom. He dreams : I know they are in Rome together,
  Looking for Antony. But all the charms of love, 20
  Salt Cleopatra, soften thy wann'd lip !
  Let witchcraft join with beauty, lust with both,
  Tie up the libertine in a field of feasts,
  Keep his brain fuming ; Epicurean cooks
  Sharpen with cloyless sauce his appetite,
  That sleep and feeding may prorogue his honour,
  Even till a Lethe'd dulness—

       Enter Varrius

        How now, Varrius !

Var. This is most certain that I shall deliver :
  Mark Antony is every hour in Rome
  Expected : since he went from Egypt 'tis   30
  A space for farther travel.

Pom.   I could have given less matter
  A better ear. Menas, I did not think
  This amorous surfeiter would have donn'd his helm
  For such a petty war : his soldiership

         28

Is twice the other twain : but let us rear
The higher our opinion, that our stirring
Can from the lap of Egypt's widow pluck
The ne'er-lust-wearied Antony.

Menas.   I cannot hope
Cæsar and Antony shall well greet together :
His wife that 's dead did trespasses to Cæsar,   40
His brother warr'd upon him, although, I think,
Not mov'd by Antony.

Pom.   I know not, Menas,
How lesser enmities may give way to greater.
Were 't not that we stand up against them all,
'Twere pregnant they should square between them-
          selves,
For they have entertained cause enough
To draw their swords : but how the fear of us
May cement their divisions, and bind up
The petty difference, we yet not know.
Be 't as our gods will have 't !   It only stands   50
Our lives upon to use our strongest hands.
Come, Menas.   *Exeunt*

SCENE II

Rome.   The house of Lepidus

Enter Enobarbus and Lepidus

Lep. Good Enobarbus, 'tis a worthy deed,
　　And shall become you well, to entreat your captain
　　To soft and gentle speech.

Eno.　　　　　　　　　　I shall entreat him
　　To answer like himself: if Cæsar move him,
　　Let Antony look over Cæsar's head,
　　And speak as loud as Mars.   By Jupiter,
　　Were I the wearer of Antonius' beard,
　　I would not shave 't to-day.

Lep.　　　　　　　　　　　'Tis not a time
　　For private stomaching.

Eno.　　　　　　　　　Every time
　　Serves for the matter that is then born in 't.　　　　　10

Lep. But small to greater matters must give way.

Eno. Not if the small come first.

Lep.　　　　　　　　　　Your speech is passion:
　　But, pray you, stir no embers up.   Here comes
　　The noble Antony.

Enter Antony and Ventidius

Eno.　　　　　　　　　And yonder, Cæsar.

30

Enter Cæsar, Mæcenas, and Agrippa

Ant. If we compose well here, to Parthia :
    Hark, Ventidius.

Cæs.   I do not know,
    Mæcenas ; ask Agrippa.

Lep.   Noble friends,
    That which combin'd us was most great, and let not
    A leaner action rend us.   What 's amiss,
    May it be gently heard.   When we debate   20
    Our trivial difference loud, we do commit
    Murder in healing wounds.   Then, noble partners,
    The rather for I earnestly beseech,
    Touch you the sourest points with sweetest terms,
    Nor curstness grow to the matter.

Ant.   'Tis spoken well.
    Were we before our armies, and to fight,
    I should do thus.   *Flourish*

Cæs. Welcome to Rome.

Ant.   Thank you.

Cæs.   Sit.

Ant.   Sit, sir.

Cæs.   Nay, then.

Ant. I learn, you take things ill which are not so :
    Or being, concern you not.

Cæs.   I must be laugh'd at,   30

If, or for nothing, or a little, I
Should say myself offended, and with you
Chiefly i' the world ; more laugh'd at, that I should
Once name you derogately, when to sound
Your name it not concern'd me.

Ant.   My being in Egypt,
Cæsar, what was 't to you ?

Cæs. No more than my residing here at Rome
Might be to you in Egypt : yet, if you there
Did practise on my state, your being in Egypt
Might be my question.

Ant.   How intend you, practis'd ?   40

Cæs. You may be pleas'd to catch at mine intent
By what did here befall me.   Your wife and brother
Made wars upon me, and their contestation   †
Was theme for you, you were the word of war.

Ant. You do mistake your business, my brother never
Did urge me in his act : I did inquire it,
And have my learning from some true reports
That drew their swords with you.   Did he not rather
Discredit my authority with yours,
And make the wars alike against my stomach,   50
Having alike your cause ? of this, my letters
Before did satisfy you.   If you 'll patch a quarrel,
As matter whole you have not to make it with,   †

It must not be with this.

Cæs.   You praise yourself
By laying defects of judgement to me, but
You patch'd up your excuses.

Ant.   Not so, not so ;
I know you could not lack, I am certain on 't,
Very necessity of this thought, that I,
Your partner in the cause 'gainst which he fought,
Could not with graceful eyes attend those wars   60
Which fronted mine own peace.   As for my wife,
I would you had her spirit in such another :
The third o' the world is yours, which with a snaffle
You may pace easy, but not such a wife.

Eno. Would we had all such wives, that the men might
go to wars with the women !

Ant. So much uncurbable, her garboils, Cæsar,
Made out of her impatience (which not wanted
Shrewdness of policy too) I grieving grant
Did you too much disquiet : for that you must   70
But say, I could not help it.

Cæs.   I wrote to you,
When rioting in Alexandria you
Did pocket up my letters ; and with taunts
Did gibe my missive out of audience.

Ant.   Sir,

33

He fell upon me ere admitted : then
Three kings I had newly feasted, and did want
Of what I was i' the morning : but next day
I told him of myself, which was as much
As to have ask'd him pardon.   Let this fellow
Be nothing of our strife ; if we contend,   80
Out of our question wipe him.

Cæs.   You have broken
The article of your oath, which you shall never
Have tongue to charge me with.

Lep.   Soft, Cæsar !

Ant. No, Lepidus, let him speak :
The honour is sacred which he talks on now,
Supposing that I lack'd it.   But on, Cæsar :
The article of my oath.

Cæs. To lend me arms, and aid when I requir'd them ;
The which you both denied.

Ant.   Neglected rather ;
And then when poison'd hours had bound me up   90
From mine own knowledge ; as nearly as I may,
I 'll play the penitent to you : but mine honesty
Shall not make poor my greatness, nor my power
Work without it.   Truth is, that Fulvia,
To have me out of Egypt, made wars here ;
For which myself, the ignorant motive, do

So far ask pardon as befits mine honour
To stoop in such a case.

Lep.   'Tis noble spoken.

Mæ. If it might please you, to enforce no further
The griefs between ye : to forget them quite   100
Were to remember that the present need
Speaks to atone you.

Lep.   Worthily spoken, Mæcenas.

Eno. Or, if you borrow one another's love for the instant,
you may, when you hear no more words of Pompey,
return it again : you shall have time to wrangle in,
when you have nothing else to do.

Ant. Thou art a soldier only : speak no more.

Eno. That truth should be silent I had almost forgot.

Ant. You wrong this presence ; therefore speak no more

Eno. Go to, then ; your considerate stone.   110

Cæs. I do not much dislike the matter, but
The manner of his speech ; for 't cannot be
We shall remain in friendship, our conditions
So differing in their acts.   Yet, if I knew
What hoop should hold us stanch, from edge to edge
O' the world I would pursue it.

Agr.   Give me leave, Cæsar.

Cæs. Speak, Agrippa.

Agr. Thou hast a sister by the mother's side,

Admir'd Octavia: great Mark Antony
Is now a widower.

Cæs.   Say not so, Agrippa: 120
If Cleopatra heard you, your reproof
Were well deserv'd of rashness.

Ant. I am not married, Cæsar: let me hear
Agrippa further speak.

Agr. To hold you in perpetual amity,
To make you brothers, and to knit your hearts
With an unslipping knot, take Antony
Octavia to his wife; whose beauty claims
No worse a husband than the best of men,
Whose virtue, and whose general graces, speak   130
That which none else can utter.   By this marriage
All little jealousies which now seem great,
And all great fears, which now import their
      dangers,
Would then be nothing: truths would be tales,   †
Where now half tales be truths: her love to both
Would each to other, and all loves to both,
Draw after her.   Pardon what I have spoke,
For 'tis a studied, not a present thought,
By duty ruminated.

Ant.   Will Cæsar speak?

Cæs. Not till he hears how Antony is touch'd   140

With what is spoke already.

Ant.   What power is in Agrippa,
If I would say, 'Agrippa, be it so,'
To make this good ?

Cæs.   The power of Cæsar, and
His power unto Octavia.

Ant.   May I never
To this good purpose, that so fairly shows,
Dream of impediment !   Let me have thy hand :
Further this act of grace ; and from this hour
The heart of brothers govern in our loves,
And sway our great designs !

Cæs.   There is my hand.
A sister I bequeath you, whom no brother   150
Did ever love so dearly.   Let her live
To join our kingdoms, and our hearts ; and never
Fly off our loves again !

Lep.   Happily, amen !

Ant. I did not think to draw my sword 'gainst Pompey,
For he hath laid strange courtesies and great
Of late upon me : I must thank him only,
Lest my remembrance suffer ill report ;
At heel of that, defy him.

Lep.   Time calls upon 's :
Of us must Pompey presently be sought,

    Or else he seeks out us.

Ant.   Where lies he ?   160

Cæs. About the Mount Misenum.

Ant.   What 's his strength
    By land ?

Cæs.   Great and increasing : but by sea
    He is an absolute master.

Ant.   So is the fame.
    Would we had spoke together !   Haste we for it :
    Yet, ere we put ourselves in arms, dispatch we
    The business we have talk'd of.

Cæs.   With most gladness,
    And do invite you to my sister's view,
    Whither straight I 'll lead you.

Ant.   Let us, Lepidus,
    Not lack your company.

Lep.   Noble Antony,
    Not sickness should detain me.   170

        Flourish.   Exeunt Cæsar, Antony, and Lepidus

Mæ. Welcome from Egypt, sir.

Eno. Half the heart of Cæsar, worthy Mæcenas !
    My honourable friend, Agrippa !

Agr. Good Enobarbus !

Mæ. We have cause to be glad that matters are so well
    digested.   You stayed well by 't in Egypt.   †

Eno. Ay, sir, we did sleep day out of countenance, and
　　made the night light with drinking.

Mæ. Eight wild-boars roasted whole at a breakfast, and
　　but twelve persons there ; is this true ?　　　　　180

Eno. This was but as a fly by an eagle : we had much
　　more monstrous matter of feast, which worthily
　　deserved noting.

Mæ. She 's a most triumphant lady, if report be square to
　　her.

Eno. When she first met Mark Antony, she purs'd up his
　　heart upon the river of Cydnus.

Agr. There she appear'd indeed, or my reporter devis'd
　　well for her.

Eno. I will tell you.　　　　　　　　　　　　　190
　　The barge she sat in, like a burnish'd throne,
　　Burn'd on the water : the poop was beaten gold,
　　Purple the sails, and so perfumed that
　　The winds were love-sick with them ; the oars were
　　　　silver,
　　Which to the tune of flutes kept stroke, and made
　　The water which they beat to follow faster,
　　As amorous of their strokes.　For her own person,
　　It beggar'd all description : she did lie
　　In her pavilion, cloth-of-gold of tissue,
　　O'er-picturing that Venus where we see　　　　　200

39

      The fancy outwork nature : on each side her
      Stood pretty dimpled boys, like smiling Cupids,
      With divers-colour'd fans, whose wind did seem
      To glow the delicate cheeks which they did
          cool,
      And what they undid did.

Agr.   O, rare for Antony !

Eno. Her gentlewomen, like the Nereides,
      So many mermaids, tended her i' the eyes,   †
      And made their bends adornings : at the helm
      A seeming mermaid steers : the silken tackle
      Swell with the touches of those flower-soft hands,   210
      That yarely frame the office. From the barge
      A strange invisible perfume hits the sense
      Of the adjacent wharfs. The city cast
      Her people out upon her ; and Antony,
      Enthron'd i' the market-place, did sit alone,
      Whistling to the air ; which, but for vacancy,
      Had gone to gaze on Cleopatra too,
      And made a gap in nature.

Agr.   Rare Egyptian !

Eno. Upon her landing, Antony sent to her,
      Invited her to supper : she replied,   220
      It should be better he became her guest,
      Which she entreated : our courteous Antony,

Whom ne'er the word of 'No' woman heard
    speak,
Being barber'd ten times o'er, goes to the feast,
And, for his ordinary, pays his heart,
For what his eyes eat only.

Agr.   Royal wench!
She made great Cæsar lay his sword to bed,
He plough'd her, and she cropp'd.

Eno.   I saw her once
Hop forty paces through the public street,
And having lost her breath, she spoke, and panted,   230
That she did make defect perfection,
And, breathless, power breathe forth.

Mæ. Now Antony must leave her utterly.

Eno. Never, he will not:
Age cannot wither her, nor custom stale
Her infinite variety: other women cloy
The appetites they feed, but she makes hungry
Where most she satisfies: for vilest things
Become themselves in her, that the holy priests
Bless her, when she is riggish.   240

Mæ. If beauty, wisdom, modesty, can settle
The heart of Antony, Octavia is
A blessed lottery to him.

Agr.   Let us go.

Good Enobarbus, make yourself my guest,
Whilst you abide here.

Eno.   Humbly, sir, I thank you.   *Exeunt*

SCENE III

The same. Cæsar's house

Enter Antony, Cæsar, Octavia between them, and Attendants

Ant. The world and my great office will sometimes
Divide me from your bosom.

Oct.   All which time
Before the gods my knee shall bow my prayers
To them for you.

Ant.   Good night, sir. My Octavia,
Read not my blemishes in the world's report :
I have not kept my square, but that to come
Shall all be done by the rule. Good night, dear lady.
Good night, sir.

Cæs. Good night.   *Exeunt all but Antony*

          Enter Lamprius

Ant. Now, sirrah ; you do wish yourself in Egypt ?   10

Lam. Would I had never come from thence, nor you
Thither !

Ant.   If you can, your reason ?

Lam.   I see it in
My motion, have it not in my tongue : but yet
Hie you to Egypt again.

Ant.   Say to me,
Whose fortunes shall rise higher, Cæsar's or mine ?

*Lam.*Cæsar's.
Therefore, O Antony, stay not by his side :
Thy demon, that thy spirit which keeps thee, is
Noble, courageous, high, unmatchable,
Where Cæsar's is not ; but near him thy angel   20
Becomes afeard, as being o'erpower'd : therefore
Make space enough between you.

Ant.   Speak this no more.

*Lam.*To none but thee ; no more but when to thee.
If thou dost play with him at any game,
Thou art sure to lose ; and, of that natural luck,
He beats thee 'gainst the odds : thy lustre thickens,
When he shines by : I say again, thy spirit
Is all afraid to govern thee near him,
But he away, 'tis noble.

Ant.   Get thee gone :
Say to Ventidius I would speak with him.   30

                              Exit Lamprius

He shall to Parthia.   Be it art or hap,
He hath spoken true : the very dice obey him,

43

And in our sports my better cunning faints
Under his chance : if we draw lots, he speeds ;
His cocks do win the battle still of mine
When it is all to nought ; and his quails ever
Beat mine, inhoop'd, at odds.   I will to Egypt :
And though I make this marriage for my peace,
I' the east my pleasure lies.

Enter Ventidius

      O, come, Ventidius,
You must to Parthia : your commission 's ready ; 40
Follow me, and receive 't.   *Exeunt*

SCENE IV

The same.   A street

Enter Lepidus, Mæcenas, and Agrippa

Lep. Trouble yourselves no further : pray you, hasten
 Your generals after.

Agr.   Sir, Mark Antony
 Will e'en but kiss Octavia, and we 'll follow.

Lep. Till I shall see you in your soldier's dress,
 Which will become you both, farewell.

Mæ.   We shall,
 As I conceive the journey, be at Mount

              †

Before you, Lepidus.

Lep.   Your way is shorter,
My purposes do draw me much about,
You 'll win two days upon me.

Mæ. }
Agr. }   Sir, good success !

Lep. Farewell.   *Exeunt*   10

SCENE V

Alexandria.   Cleopatra's palace

Enter Cleopatra, Charmian, Iras, and Alexas

Cle. Give me some music ; music, moody food
Of us that trade in love.

All.   The music, ho !

Enter Mardian

Cle. Let it alone, let 's to billiards : come, Charmian.

Cha. My arm is sore, best play with Mardian.

Cle. As well a woman with an eunuch play'd
As with a woman. Come, you 'll play with me, sir ?

Mar. As well as I can, madam.

Cle. And when good will is show'd, though 't come too
        short,
The actor may plead pardon.   I 'll none now ;

45

Give me mine angle, we'll to the river there,   10
My music playing far off; I will betray
Tawny-finn'd fishes, my bended hook shall pierce
Their slimy jaws; and as I draw them up,
I'll think them every one an Antony,
And say 'Ah, ha! you're caught.'

Cha.   'Twas merry when
You wager'd on your angling, when your diver
Did hang a salt-fish on his hook, which he
With fervency drew up.

Cle.   That time? O times!
I laugh'd him out of patience, and that night
I laugh'd him into patience, and next morn,   20
Ere the ninth hour, I drunk him to his bed;
Then put my tires and mantles on him, whilst
I wore his sword Philippan.

Enter a Messenger

                O, from Italy!
Ram thou thy fruitful tidings in mine ears,
That long time have been barren.

Mes.   Madam, madam,—

Cle. Antonius dead! If thou say so, villain,
Thou kill'st thy mistress: but well and free,
If thou so yield him, there is gold, and here
My bluest veins to kiss: a hand that kings

Have lipp'd, and trembled kissing.

Mes. First, madam, he is well.

Cle.   Why, there 's more gold.
But, sirrah, mark, we use
To say the dead are well : bring it to that,
The gold I give thee will I melt and pour
Down thy ill-uttering throat.

Mes. Good madam, hear me.

Cle.   Well, go to, I will ;
But there 's no goodness in thy face, if Antony
Be free and healthful,—so tart a favour
To trumpet such good tidings !   If not well,
Thou shouldst come like a Fury crown'd with snakes, 40
Not like a formal man.

Mes.   Will 't please you hear me ?

Cle. I have a mind to strike thee ere thou speak'st :
Yet, if thou say Antony lives, is well,
Or friends with Cæsar, or not captive to him,
I 'll set thee in a shower of gold, and hail
Rich pearls upon thee.

Mes.   Madam, he 's well.

Cle.   Well said.

Mes. And friends with Cæsar.

Cle.   Thou 'rt an honest man.

Mes. Cæsar, and he, are greater friends than ever.

Cle. Make thee a fortune from me.

Mes.   But yet, madam,—

Cle. I do not like ' But yet,' it does allay   50
    The good precedence, fie upon ' But yet ' !
    ' But yet ' is as a gaoler to bring forth
    Some monstrous malefactor.   Prithee, friend,
    Pour out the pack of matter to mine ear,
    The good and bad together : he 's friends with Cæsar,
    In state of health, thou say'st, and, thou say'st, free.

Mes. Free, madam ! no ; I made no such report,
    He 's bound unto Octavia.

Cle.   For what good turn ?

Mes. For the best turn i' the bed.

Cle.   I am pale, Charmian.

Mes. Madam, he 's married to Octavia.   60

Cle. The most infectious pestilence upon thee !

                                        Strikes him down

Mes. Good madam, patience.

Cle.   What say you ?   Hence,

                                        Strikes him again

    Horrible villain, or I 'll spurn thine eyes
    Like balls before me ; I 'll unhair thy head,

                                She hales him up and down

    Thou shalt be whipp'd with wire, and stew'd in brine,
    Smarting in lingering pickle.

48

Mes.   Gracious madam,
　I that do bring the news made not the match.

Cle. Say 'tis not so, a province I will give thee,
　And make thy fortunes proud : the blow thou hadst
　Shall make thy peace, for moving me to rage,   70
　And I will boot thee with what gift beside
　Thy modesty can beg.

Mes.   He 's married, madam.

Cle. Rogue, thou hast liv'd too long.   *Draws a knife*

Mes.   Nay, then I 'll run.
　What mean you madam ? I have made no fault.   *Exit*

Cha. Good madam, keep yourself within yourself,
　The man is innocent.

Cle. Some innocents 'scape not the thunderbolt.
　Melt Egypt into Nile ! and kindly creatures
　Turn all to serpents !   Call the slave again,
　Though I am mad, I will not bite him : call.   80

Cha. He is afeard to come.

Cle.   I will not hurt him,

　　　　　　　　　　　　Exit Charmian

　These hands do lack nobility, that they strike
　A meaner than myself ; since I myself
　Have given myself the cause.

　　　　　Re-enter Charmian and Messenger

　　　　　　　　　　Come hither, sir.

　　　　　　　　　49

Though it be honest, it is never good
To bring bad news : give to a gracious message
An host of tongues, but let ill tidings tell
Themselves when they be felt.

Mes.   I have done my duty.

Cle. Is he married ?
I cannot hate thee worser than I do,   90
If thou again say ' Yes.'

Mes.   He 's married, madam.

Cle. The gods confound thee ! dost thou hold there still ?

Mes. Should I lie, madam ?

Cle.   O, I would thou didst,
So half my Egypt were submerg'd and made
A cistern for scal'd snakes !   Go get thee hence,
Hadst thou Narcissus in thy face, to me
Thou wouldst appear most ugly.   He is married ?

Mes. I crave your highness' pardon.

Cle.   He is married ?

Mes. Take no offence that I would not offend you :
To punish me for what you make me do   100
Seems much unequal : he 's married to Octavia.

Cle. O, that his fault should make a knave of thee,
That art not what thou 'rt sure of !   Get thee hence :   †
The merchandise which thou hast brought from
    Rome

50

    Are all too dear for me : lie they upon thy hand,
    And be undone by 'em !   *Exit Messenger*

Cha.   Good your highness, patience.

Cle. In praising Antony, I have disprais'd Cæsar.

Cha. Many times, madam.

Cle.   I am paid for 't now.
    Lead me from hence,
    I faint : O Iras, Charmian ! 'tis no matter.   110
    Go to the fellow, good Alexas ; bid him
    Report the feature of Octavia ; her years,
    Her inclination, let him not leave out
    The colour of her hair : bring me word quickly.
                           Exit Alexas
    Let him for ever go, let him not, Charmian,
    Though he be painted one way like a Gorgon,
    The other way's a Mars.   *(to Mardian)* Bid you
        Alexas
    Bring me word how tall she is.   Pity me, Charmian,
    But do not speak to me.   Lead me to my chamber.
                               Exeunt

SCENE VI

Near Misenum

Flourish.   Enter Pompey and Menas from one side, with drum
    and trumpet : at another, Cæsar, Antony, Lepidus,
    Enobarbus, Mæcenas, Agrippa, with Soldiers marching.

Pom. Your hostages I have, so have you mine ;
   And we shall talk before we fight.

Cæs.   Most meet
   The first we come to words, and therefore have we
   Our written purposes before us sent,
   Which, if thou hast consider'd, let us know
   If 'twill tie up thy discontented sword,
   And carry back to Sicily much tall youth,
   That else must perish here.

Pom.   To you all three,
   The senators alone of this great world,
   Chief factors for the gods, I do not know   10
   Wherefore my father should revengers want,
   Having a son and friends, since Julius Cæsar,
   Who at Philippi the good Brutus ghosted,
   There saw you labouring for him.   What was 't
   That mov'd pale Cassius to conspire ? and what
   Made the all-honour'd honest Roman, Brutus,

With the arm'd rest, courtiers of beauteous freedom,
To drench the Capitol, but that they would
Have one man but a man?   And that is it
Hath made me rig my navy, at whose burthen   20
The anger'd ocean foams, with which I meant
To scourge the ingratitude that despiteful Rome
Cast on my noble father.

Cæs.   Take your time.

Ant. Thou canst not fear us, Pompey, with thy sails;
We'll speak with thee at sea: at land, thou know'st
How much we do o'ercount thee.

Pom.   At land indeed
Thou dost o'ercount me of my father's house:
But since the cuckoo builds not for himself,
Remain in't as thou mayst.

Lep.   Be pleas'd to tell us
(For this is from the present) how you take   30
The offers we have sent you.

Cæs.   There's the point.

Ant. Which do not be entreated to, but weigh
What it is worth embrac'd.

Cæs.   And what may follow,
To try a larger fortune.

Pom.   You have made me offer
Of Sicily, Sardinia; and I must

Rid all the sea of pirates ; then, to send
Measures of wheat to Rome ; this 'greed upon,
To part with unhack'd edges, and bear back
Our targes undinted.

Cæs.
Ant.   That 's our offer.
Lep.

Pom.   Know then,
I came before you here a man prepar'd   40
To take this offer : but Mark Antony
Put me to some impatience : though I lose
The praise of it by telling : you must know,
When Cæsar and your brother were at blows,
Your mother came to Sicily and did find
Her welcome friendly.

Ant.   I have heard it, Pompey,
And am well studied for a liberal thanks,
Which I do owe you.

Pom.   Let me have your hand :
I did not think, sir, to have met you here.

Ant. The beds i' the east are soft, and thanks to you,   50
That call'd me timelier than my purpose hither ;
For I have gain'd by 't.

Cæs.   Since I saw you last,
There is a change upon you.

Pom.   Well, I know not
    What counts harsh fortune casts upon my face ;
    But in my bosom shall she never come,
    To make my heart her vassal.

Lep.   Well met here.

Pom. I hope so, Lepidus.   Thus we are agreed :
    I crave our composition may be written
    And seal'd between us.

Cæs.   That 's the next to do.

Pom. We 'll feast each other ere we part, and let 's   60
    Draw lots who shall begin.

Ant.   That will I, Pompey.

Pom. No, Antony, take the lot :
    But, first or last, your fine Egyptian cookery
    Shall have the fame.   I have heard that Julius
        Cæsar
    Grew fat with feasting there.

Ant.   You have heard much.

Pom. I have fair meaning, sir.

Ant.   And fair words to them.

Pom. Then so much have I heard :
    And I have heard, Apollodorus carried—

Eno. No more of that : he did so.

Pom.   What, I pray you ?

Eno. A certain queen to Cæsar in a mattress.   70

Pom. I know thee now, how far'st thou, soldier?

Eno.   Well;

    And well am like to do, for I perceive

    Four feasts are toward.

Pom.   Let me shake thy hand,

    I never hated thee: I have seen thee fight,

    When I have envied thy behaviour.

Eno.   Sir,

    I never lov'd you much, but I ha' prais'd ye,

    When you have well deserv'd ten times as much

    As I have said you did.

Pom.   Enjoy thy plainness,

    It nothing ill becomes thee.

    Aboard my galley I invite you all: 80

    Will you lead, lords?

Cæs. ⎫

Ant. ⎬   Show us the way, sir.

Lep. ⎭

Pom.   Come.

                Exeunt all but Menas and Enobarbus

Menas. (*aside*) Thy father, Pompey, would ne'er have
    made this treaty.—You and I have known, sir.

Eno. At sea, I think.

Menas. We have, sir.

Eno. You have done well by water.

Menas. And you by land.

Eno. I will praise any man that will praise me; though
    it cannot be denied what I have done by land.

Menas. Nor what I have done by water.   90

Eno. Yes, something you can deny for your own safety:
    you have been a great thief by sea.

Menas. And you by land.

Eno. There I deny my land service: but give me your
    hand, Menas, if our eyes had authority, here they
    might take two thieves kissing.

Menas. All men's faces are true, whatsoe'er their hands are.

Eno. But there is never a fair woman has a true face.

Menas. No slander, they steal hearts.

Eno. We came hither to fight with you.   100

Menas. For my part, I am sorry it is turn'd to a drinking.
    Pompey doth this day laugh away his fortune.

Eno. If he do, sure he cannot weep 't back again.

Menas. You 've said, sir; we looked not for Mark Antony
    here: pray you, is he married to Cleopatra?

Eno. Cæsar's sister is called Octavia.

Menas. True, sir; she was the wife of Caius Marcellus.

Eno. But she is now the wife of Marcus Antonius.

Menas. Pray ye, sir?

Eno. 'Tis true.   110

Menas. Then is Cæsar and he for ever knit together.

Eno. If I were bound to divine of this unity, I would not
    prophesy so.

Menas. I think the policy of that purpose made more in
    the marriage than the love of the parties.

Eno. I think so too. But you shall find, the band that
    seems to tie their friendship together will be the very
    strangler of their amity : Octavia is of a holy, cold,
    and still conversation.

Menas. Who would not have his wife so ?   120

Eno. Not he that himself is not so ; which is Mark
    Antony. He will to his Egyptian dish again : then
    shall the sighs of Octavia blow the fire up in Cæsar ;
    and (as I said before) that which is the strength of
    their amity shall prove the immediate author of
    their variance. Antony will use his affection where
    it is : he married but his occasion here.

Menas. And thus it may be. Come, sir, will you aboard ?
    I have a health for you.

Eno. I shall take it, sir : we have us'd our throats in 130
    Egypt.

Menas. Come, let 's away.   *Exeunt*

SCENE VII

On board Pompey's galley, off Misenum

Music plays. Enter two or three Servants, with a banquet

1.*S.* Here they'll be, man. Some o' their plants are
ill-rooted already ; the least wind i' the world will
blow them down.

2.*S.* Lepidus is high-coloured.

1.*S.* They have made him drink alms-drink.

2.*S.* As they pinch one another by the disposition, he
cries out ' No more ; ' reconciles them to his entreaty,
and himself to the drink.

1.*S.* But it raises the greater war between him and his
discretion.   10

2.*S.* Why, this it is to have a name in great men's fellow-
ship : I had as lief have a reed that will do me no
service as a partisan I could not heave.

1.*S.* To be call'd into a huge sphere, and not to be seen
to move in 't, are the holes where eyes should be,
which pitifully disaster the cheeks.

*A sennet sounded. Enter Cæsar, Antony, Pompey, Lepidus,
Agrippa, Mæcenas, Enobarbus, Menas, with other
captains.*

Ant.(*to Cæsar*) Thus do they, sir: they take the flow o' the Nile

By certain scales i' the pyramid ; they know
By the height, the lowness, or the mean, if dearth
Or foison follow : the higher Nilus swells,   20
The more it promises : as it ebbs, the seedsman
Upon the slime and ooze scatters his grain,
And shortly comes to harvest.

Lep. You 've strange serpents there ?

Ant. Ay, Lepidus.

Lep. Your serpent of Egypt is bred now of your mud by
    the operation of your sun : so is your crocodile.

Ant. They are so.

Pom. Sit, and some wine !   A health to Lepidus !

Lep. I am not so well as I should be, but I 'll ne'er out.   30

Eno. Not till you have slept ; I fear me you 'll be in till
    then.

Lep. Nay, certainly, I have heard the Ptolemies pyramises
    are very goodly things ; without contradiction, I
    have heard that.

Menas. (*aside to Pom.*) Pompey, a word.

Pom.   (*aside to Menas*) Say in mine ear, what is 't ?

Menas. (*aside to Pom.*) Forsake thy seat, I do beseech thee,
      captain.

And hear me speak a word.

Pom.   (*aside to Menas*) Forbear me till anon.—
This wine for Lepidus.

Lep. What manner o' thing is your crocodile ?   40

Ant. It is shap'd, sir, like itself, and it is as broad as it hath
    breadth ; it is just so high as it is, and moves with it
    own organs : it lives by that which nourisheth it,
    and the elements once out of it, it transmigrates.

Lep. What colour is it of ?

Ant. Of it own colour too.

Lep. 'Tis a strange serpent.

Ant. 'Tis so, and the tears of it are wet.

Cæs. Will this description satisfy him ?

Ant. With the health that Pompey gives him, else he is a   50
    very epicure.

Pom. Go hang, sir, hang !   Tell me of that ? away !
    Do as I bid you.   Where 's this cup I call'd for ?

Menas. (*aside to Pom.*) If for the sake of merit thou wilt
        hear me,
    Rise from thy stool.

Pom. (*aside to Menas*) I think thou 'rt mad.   The matter ?
                    Rises, and walks aside

Menas. I have ever held my cap off to thy fortunes.

Pom. Thou hast serv'd me with much faith.   What 's else
        to say ?
    Be jolly, lords.

Ant.   These quick-sands, Lepidus,
    Keep off them, for you sink.   60

61

Menas. Wilt thou be lord of all the world ?

Pom. What say'st thou ?

Menas. Wilt thou be lord of the whole world ?   That's
  twice.

Pom. How should that be ?

Menas. But entertain it,
 And, though thou think me poor, I am the man
 Will give thee all the world.

Pom. Hast thou drunk well ?

Menas. No, Pompey, I have kept me from the cup.
 Thou art, if thou dar'st be, the earthly Jove :
 Whate'er the ocean pales, or sky inclips,
 Is thine, if thou wilt ha 't.

Pom. Show me which way.

Menas. These three world-sharers, these competitors, 70
 Are in thy vessel : let me cut the cable,
 And, when we are put off, fall to their throats :
 All there is thine.

Pom. Ah, this thou shouldst have done,
 And not have spoke on 't ! In me 'tis villany ;
 In thee 't had been good service. Thou must know,
 'Tis not my profit that does lead mine honour ;
 Mine honour, it.   Repent that e'er thy tongue
 Hath so betray'd thine act : being done unknown,
 I should have found it afterwards well done,

But must condemn it now. Desist, and drink. 80

Menas. (*aside*) For this,
  I 'll never follow thy pall'd fortunes more ;
  Who seeks, and will not take when once 'tis offer'd,
  Shall never find it more.

Pom.   This health to Lepidus !

Ant. Bear him ashore, I 'll pledge it for him, Pompey.

Eno. Here 's to thee, Menas !

Menas.   Enobarbus, welcome !

Pom. Fill till the cup be hid.

Eno. There 's a strong fellow, Menas.

    Pointing to the Attendant who carries off Lepidus

Menas. Why ?

Eno. A' bears the third part of the world, man ; see'st
  not ? 90

Menas. The third part then he is drunk : would it were
  all,
  That it might go on wheels !

Eno. Drink thou ; increase the reels.

Menas. Come.

Pom. This is not yet an Alexandrian feast.

Ant. It ripens towards it. Strike the vessels, ho ! †
  Here 's to Cæsar !

Cæs.   I could well forbear 't ;
  It 's monstrous labour, when I wash my brain

 18 *f*   63

  And it grows fouler.

Ant.   Be a child o' the time.

Cæs. Possess it, I'll make answer: 100
  But I had rather fast from all four days
  Than drink so much in one.

Eno.   (*to Antony*) Ha, my brave emperor,
  Shall we dance now the Egyptian Bacchanals,
  And celebrate our drink?

Pom. Let's ha't, good soldier.

Ant. Come, let's all take hands,
  Till that the conquering wine hath steep'd our
    sense
  In soft and delicate Lethe.

Eno.   All take hands.
  Make battery to our ears with the loud music,
  The while I'll place you, then the boy shall sing; 110
  The holding every man shall bear as loud
  As his strong sides can volley.

    Music plays. Enobarbus places them hand in hand

THE SONG

  Come, thou monarch of the vine,
  Plumpy Bacchus, with pink eyne!
  In thy fats our cares be drown'd,
  With thy grapes our hairs be crown'd:

        Cup us till the world go round,

        Cup us till the world go round !

Cæs. What would you more ?   Pompey, good night.

        Good brother,

    Let me request you off : our graver business   120

    Frowns at this levity.   Gentle lords, let 's part ;

    You see we have burnt our cheeks : strong Enobarb

    Is weaker than the wine, and mine own tongue

    Splits what it speaks : the wild disguise hath

        almost   †

    Antick'd us all.   What needs more words ?   Good

        night.

    Good Antony, your hand.

Pom.   I 'll try you on the shore.

Ant. And shall, sir : give 's your hand.

Pom.   O Antony,

    You have my father's house,—But, what ? we are

        friends.

    Come, down into the boat.

Eno.   Take heed you fall not.

                Exeunt all but Enobarbus and Menas

    Menas, I 'll not on shore.

Menas.   No, to my cabin.   130

    These drums ! these trumpets, flutes ! what !

    Let Neptune hear we bid a loud farewell

To these great fellows : sound and be hang'd, sound
out !   *Sound a flourish, with drums*

Eno. Hoo ! says a'. There 's my cap.   †

Menas. Ho ! Noble captain, come.   *Exeunt*

Act Third

SCENE I

A plain in Syria

*Enter Ventidius as it were in triumph, with Silius, and other
Romans, Officers, and soldiers ; the dead body of Pacorus
borne before him*

Ven. Now, darting Parthia, art thou struck and now
Pleas'd fortune does of Marcus Crassus' death
Make me revenger. Bear the king's son's body
Before our army. Thy Pacorus, Orodes,
Pays this for Marcus Crassus.

Sil.   Noble Ventidius,
Whilst yet with Parthian blood thy sword is warm
The fugitive Parthians follow ; spur through Media,
Mesopotamia, and the shelters whither
The routed fly : so thy grand captain Antony

Shall set thee on triumphant chariots, and   10
Put garlands on thy head.

Ven.   O Silius, Silius,
I have done enough : a lower place, note well
May make too great an act ; for learn this, Silius,
Better to leave undone than by our deed
Acquire too high a fame when him we serve 's away.
Cæsar and Antony have ever won
More in their officer than person : Sossius,
One of my place in Syria, his lieutenant,
For quick accumulation of renown,
Which he achiev'd by the minute, lost his favour.   20
Who does i' the wars more then his captain can
Becomes his captain's captain : and ambition
(The soldier's virtue) rather makes choice of loss
Than gain which darkens him.
I could do more to do Antonius good,
But 'twould offend him ; and in his offence
Should my performance perish.

Sil.   Thou hast, Ventidius, that
Without the which a soldier and his sword
Grants   scarce   distinction.   Thou   wilt   write   to
     Antony ?

Ven. I 'll humbly signify what in his name,   30
That magical word of war, we have effected,

How, with his banners and his well-paid ranks,
The ne'er-yet-beaten horse of Parthia
We have jaded out o' the field.

Sil.   Where is he now ?

Ven. He purposeth to Athens, whither, with what haste
The weight we must convey with's will permit,
We shall appear before him.   On, there, pass along !

                                  Exeunt

SCENE II

Rome.   An ante-chamber in Cæsar's house

Enter Agrippa at one door, and Enobarbus at another

Agr. What, are the brothers parted ?

Eno. They have dispatch'd with Pompey ; he is gone ;
The other three are sealing.   Octavia weeps
To part from Rome ; Cæsar is sad, and Lepidus
Since Pompey's feast, as Menas says, is troubled
With the green sickness.   †

Agr.   'Tis a noble Lepidus.

Eno. A very fine one : O, how he loves Cæsar !

Agr. Nay, but how dearly he adores Mark Antony !

Eno. Cæsar ?   Why, he's the Jupiter of men.

Agr. What's Antony ?   The god of Jupiter.   10

Eno. Spake you of Cæsar?   How! the nonpareil!

Agr. O Antony, O thou Arabian bird!

Eno. Would you praise Cæsar, say ' Cæsar ' : go no further.

Agr. Indeed, he plied them both with excellent praises.

Eno. But he loves Cæsar best, yet he loves Antony :

    Ho ! hearts, tongues, figures, scribes, bards, poets,
      cannot

    Think, speak, cast, write, sing, number—hoo !—

    His love to Antony.   But as for Cæsar,

    Kneel down, kneel down, and wonder.

Agr.   Both he loves.

Eno. They are his shards, and he their beetle. (*Trumpet
    within.*) So ;   20

    This is to horse.   Adieu, noble Agrippa.

Agr. Good fortune, worthy soldier, and farewell.

        Enter Cæsar, Antony, Lepidus, and Octavia

Ant. No further, sir.

Cæs. You take from me a great part of myself ;

    Use me well in 't.   Sister, prove such a wife

    As my thoughts make thee, and as my farthest band

    Shall pass on thy approof.   Most noble Antony,

    Let not the piece of virtue which is set

    Betwixt us, as the cement of our love,

    To keep it builded, be the ram to batter   30

    The fortress of it ; for better might we

Have lov'd without this mean, if on both parts
This be not cherish'd.

Ant.　　　　　　　　Make me not offended
In your distrust.

Cæs.　　　　　I have said.

Ant.　　　　　　　　You shall not find,
Though you be therein curious, the least cause
For what you seem to fear : so, the gods keep you,
And make the hearts of Romans serve your ends !
We will here part.

Cæs. Farewell, my dearest sister, fare thee well,
The elements be kind to thee, and make　　　　40
Thy spirits all of comfort ! fare thee well.

Oct. My noble brother !

Ant. The April's in her eyes, it is love's spring,
And these the showers to bring it on.　Be cheerful.

Oct. Sir, look well to my husband's house, and—

Cæs.　　　　　　　　　　　　What,
Octavia ?

Oct. I 'll tell you in your ear.

Ant. Her tongue will not obey her heart, nor can
Her heart inform her tongue, the swan's down-feather,
That stands upon the swell at full of tide　　　50
And neither way inclines.

Eno.　　　　(aside to Agr.) Will Cæsar weep ?

Agr.　　　　　*(aside to Eno.)* He has a cloud in's face.

Eno. (aside to Agr.) He were the worse for that, were he
　　　a horse ;

So is he, being a man.

Agr.　　　　*(aside to Eno.)* Why, Enobarbus,

When Antony found Julius Cæsar dead,

He cried almost to roaring ; and he wept

When at Philippi he found Brutus slain.

Eno. (aside to Agr.) That year indeed he was troubled with
　　　a rheum ;

What willingly he did confound he wail'd,

Believe 't, till I wept too.

Cæs.　　　　　　　　No, sweet Octavia,

You shall hear from me still ; the time shall not　　60

Out-go my thinking on you.

Ant.　　　　　　　　Come, sir, come ;

I 'll wrestle with you in my strength of love :

Look, here I have you, thus I let you go,

And give you to the gods.

Cæs.　　　　　　　　Adieu, be happy !

Lep. Let all the number of the stars give light

To thy fair way !

Cæs.　　　　　Farewell, farewell !　*Kisses Octavia*

Ant.　　　　　　　　Farewell !

　　　　　　　Trumpets sound.　Exeunt

71

SCENE III

Alexandria.   Cleopatra's palace

Enter Cleopatra, Charmian, Iras, and Alexas

Cle. Where is the fellow?

Al.   Half afeard to come.

Cle. Go to, go to.

Enter the Messenger as before

Come hither, sir.

Al.   Good majesty,
Herod of Jewry dare not look upon you
But when you are well pleas'd.

Cle.   That Herod's head
I 'll have: but how?   When Antony is gone
Through whom I might command it?   Come thou
          near.

Mes. Most gracious majesty,—

Cle.   Didst thou behold
Octavia?

Mes.   Ay, dread queen.

Cle.   Where?

Mes.   Madam, in Rome:
I look'd her in the face, and saw her led
Between her brother and Mark Antony.   10

72

Cle. Is she as tall as me ?

Mes.   She is not, madam.

Cle. Didst hear her speak ? is she shrill-tongu'd or low ?

Mes. Madam, I heard her speak ; she is low-voic'd.

Cle. That 's not so good ; he cannot like her long.

Cha. Like her !   O Isis ! 'tis impossible.

Cle. I think so, Charmian : dull of tongue, and dwarfish.
     What majesty is in her gait ?   Remember,
     If e'er thou look'dst on majesty.

Mes.   She creeps :
     Her motion and her station are as one ;
     She shows a body, rather than a life,   20
     A statue than a breather.

Cle.   Is this certain ?

Mes. Or I have no observance.

Cha.   Three in Egypt
     Cannot make better note.

Cle.   He 's very knowing,
     I do perceive 't : there 's nothing in her yet :
     The fellow has good judgment.

Cha.   Excellent.

Cle. Guess at her years, I prithee.

Mes.   Madam,
     She was a widow—

Cle.   Widow ?   Charmian, hark.

Mes. And I do think she's thirty.

Cle. Bear'st thou her face in mind? is't long or round?

Mes. Round, even to faultiness.   30

Cle. For the most part, too, they are foolish that are so.
    Her hair what colour?

Mes.   Brown, madam: and her forehead
    As low as she would wish it.

Cle.   There's gold for thee.
    Thou must not take my former sharpness ill:
    I will employ thee back again; I find thee
    Most fit for business: go make thee ready;
    Our letters are prepar'd.   *Exit Messenger*

Cha.   A proper man.

Cle. Indeed, he is so: I repent me much
    That so I harried him.   Why, methinks, by him,
    This creature's no such thing.

Cha.   Nothing, madam.   40

Cle. The man hath seen some majesty, and should know.

Cha. Hath he seen majesty?   Isis else defend;
    And serving you so long!

Cle. I have one thing more to ask him yet, good
        Charmian:
    But 'tis no matter, thou shalt bring him to me
    Where I will write; all may be well enough.

Cha. I warrant you, madam.   *Exeunt*

SCENES IV AND V

Athens.   Antony's house

Enter Antony and Octavia

Ant. Nay, nay, Octavia, not only that,
That were excusable, that and thousands more
Of semblable import, but he hath wag'd
New wars 'gainst Pompey ; made his will, and read it
To public ear,
Spoke scantly of me : when perforce he could not
But pay me terms of honour, cold and sickly
He vented them ; most narrow measure lent me ;
When the best hint was given him, he not took 't,
Or did it from his teeth.

Oct.   O my good lord,   10
Believe not all, or, if you must believe,
Stomach not all.   A more unhappy lady,
If this division chance, ne'er stood between,
Praying for both parts :
The good gods will mock me presently,
When I shall pray, ' O, bless my lord and husband ! '
Undo that prayer, by crying out as loud,
' O, bless my brother ! '   Husband win, win brother,
Prays, and destroys the prayer ; no midway

75

'Twixt these extremes at all.

Ant.   Gentle Octavia.   20

Let your best love draw to that point, which seeks
Best to preserve it ; if I lose mine honour,
I lose myself : better I were not yours
Than yours so branchless.   But, as you requested,
Yourself shall go between 's : the mean time, lady,
I 'll raise the preparation of a war
Shall stain your brother : make your soonest haste ;
So your desires are yours.

Oct.   Thanks to my lord.

The Jove of power make me, most weak, most weak,
Your reconciler !   Wars 'twixt you twain would be   30
As if the world should cleave, and that slain men
Should solder up the rift.

Ant. When it appears to you where this begins,
Turn your displeasure that way, for our faults
Can never be so equal, that your love
Can equally move with them.   Provide your going,
Choose your own company, and command what cost
Your heart has mind to.   *Exeunt*

Enter Enobarbus and Eros, meeting

Eno. How now, friend Eros ?

Er. There 's strange news come, sir.

Eno. What, man?

Er. Cæsar and Lepidus have made wars upon Pompey.

Eno. This is old: what is the success?

Er. Cæsar, having made use of him in the wars 'gainst
    Pompey, presently denied him rivality, would not
    let him partake in the glory of the action, and not
    resting here, accuses him of letters he had formerly
    wrote to Pompey; upon his own appeal, seizes him: 10
    so the poor third is up, till death enlarge his confine.

Eno. Then, world, thou hast a pair of chaps, no more;
    And throw between them all the food thou hast,
    They 'll grind the one the other.   Where 's Antony?

Er. He 's walking in the garden—thus; and spurns
    The rush that lies before him; cries 'Fool Lepidus!' †
    And threats the throat of that his officer
    That murder'd Pompey.

Eno.   Our great navy 's rigg'd.

Er. For Italy and Cæsar.   More, Domitius,
    My lord desires you presently: my news   20
    I might have told hereafter.

Eno.   'Twill be naught,
    But let it be.   Bring me to Antony.

Er. Come, sir.   *Exeunt*

SCENE VI

Rome.   Cæsar's house

Enter Cæsar, Agrippa, and Mæcenas

Cæs. Contemning Rome, he has done all this, and more,
    In Alexandria : here's the manner of 't :
    I' the market-place, on a tribunal silver'd,
    Cleopatra and himself in chairs of gold
    Were publicly enthron'd : at the feet sat
    Cæsarion, whom they call my father's son,
    And all the unlawful issue that their lust
    Since then hath made between them.   Unto her
    He gave the stablishment of Egypt, made her
    Of lower Syria, Cyprus, Lydia,   10
    Absolute queen.

Mæ.   This in the public eye ?

Cæs. I' the common show-place, where they exercise.
    His sons he there proclaim'd the kings of kings :
    Great Media, Parthia, and Armenia,
    He gave to Alexander ; to Ptolemy he assign'd
    Syria, Cilicia and Phœnicia : she
    In the habiliments of the goddess Isis
    That day appear'd, and oft before gave audience,
    As 'tis reported, so.

Mæ.   Let Rome be thus
  Inform'd.

Agr.   Who, queasy with his insolence   20
  Already, will their good thoughts call from him.

Cæs. The people knows it, and have now receiv'd
  His accusations.

Agr.   Who does he accuse ?

Cæs. Cæsar, and that, having in Sicily
  Sextus Pompeius spoil'd, we had not rated him
  His part o' the isle : then does he say, he lent me
  Some shipping unrestor'd : lastly, he frets
  That Lepidus of the triumvirate
  Should be depos'd ; and, being, that we detain
  All his revenue.

Agr.   Sir, this should be answer'd.   30

Cæs. 'Tis done already, and the messenger gone.
  I have told him, Lepidus was grown too cruel,
  That he his high authority abus'd
  And did deserve his change : for what I have con-
      quer'd,
  I grant him part ; but then, in his Armenia
  And other of his conquer'd kingdoms, I
  Demand the like.

Mæ.   He 'll never yield to that.

Cæs. Nor must not then be yielded to in this.

Enter Octavia, with her train

Oct. Hail, Cæsar, and my lord ! hail, most dear Cæsar !

Cæs. That ever I should call thee castaway !   40

Oct. You have not call'd me so, nor have you cause.

Cæs. Why have you stol'n upon us thus ?   You come not
    Like Cæsar's sister : the wife of Antony
    Should have an army for an usher, and
    The neighs of horse to tell of her approach,
    Long ere she did appear ; the trees by the way
    Should have borne men, and expectation fainted,
    Longing for what it had not ; nay, the dust
    Should have ascended to the roof of heaven,
    Rais'd by your populous troops : but you are come   50
    A market-maid to Rome, and have prevented
    The ostentation of our love ; which, left unshown,
    Is often left unlov'd : we should have met you
    By sea and land, supplying every stage
    With an augmented greeting.

Oct.   Good my lord,
    To come thus was I not constrain'd, but did it
    On my free will.   My lord, Mark Antony,
    Hearing that you prepar'd for war, acquainted
    My grieved ear withal ; whereon, I begg'd
    His pardon for return.

Cæs.   Which soon he granted,   60

　　　Being an obstruct 'tween his lust and him.

Oct. Do not say so, my lord.

Cæs.　　　　　　　　　I have eyes upon him,
　　　And his affairs come to me on the wind.
　　　Where is he now ?

Oct.　　　　　　　My lord, in Athens.

Cæs. No, my most wronged sister, Cleopatra
　　　Hath nodded him to her.　He hath given his empire
　　　Up to a whore, who now are levying
　　　The kings o' the earth for war : he hath assembled
　　　Bocchus, the king of Libya, Archelaus,
　　　Of Cappadocia, Philadelphos king　　　　　　70
　　　Of Paphlagonia, the Thracian king Adallas,
　　　King Malchus of Arabia, King of Pont,
　　　Herod of Jewry, Mithridates king
　　　Of Comagene, Polemon and Amyntas,
　　　The kings of Mede and Lycaonia,
　　　With a more larger list of sceptres.

Oct.　　　　　　　　　Ay me most wretched,
　　　That have my heart parted betwixt two friends
　　　That does afflict each other !

Cæs.　　　　　　　　Welcome hither :
　　　Your letters did withhold our breaking forth,
　　　Till we perceiv'd both how you were wrong led　　80
　　　And we in negligent danger.　Cheer your heart,

Be you not troubled with the time, which drives
O 'er your content these strong necessities,
But let determin'd things to destiny
Hold unbewail'd their way.   Welcome to Rome,
Nothing more dear to me.   You are abus'd
Beyond the mark of thought : and the high gods,
To do you justice, make their ministers
Of us, and those that love you.   Best of comfort,
And ever welcome to us.

Agr.   Welcome, lady.   90

Mæ. Welcome, dear madam,
Each heart in Rome does love and pity you,
Only the adulterous Antony, most large
In his abominations, turns you off ;
And gives his potent regiment to a trull,
That noises it against us.

Oct.   Is it so, sir ?

Cæs. Most certain.   Sister, welcome : pray you,
Be ever known to patience : my dear'st sister !

                                             Exeunt

SCENE VII

Near Actium.   Antony's camp

Enter Cleopatra and Enobarbus

Cle. I will be even with thee, doubt it not.

Eno. But why, why, why?

Cle. Thou hast forspoke my being in these wars,
And say'st it is not fit.

Eno.   Well, is it, is it?

Cle. If not denounc'd against us, why should not we   †
Be there in person?

Eno.   (*aside*) Well, I could reply:
If we should serve with horse and mares together,   †
The horse were merely lost; the mares would bear
A soldier and his horse.

Cle.   What is't you say?

Eno. Your presence needs must puzzle Antony;   10
Take from his heart, take from his brain, from 's time,
What should not then be spar'd.   He is already
Traduc'd for levity, and 'tis said in Rome
That Photinus, an eunuch, and your maids
Manage this war.

Cle.   Sink Rome, and their tongues rot
That speak against us!   A charge we bear i' the war,

83

And, as the president of my kingdom, will
Appear there for a man.   Speak not against it,
I will not stay behind.

Eno.   Nay, I have done ;
Here comes the emperor.

Enter Antony and Canidius

Ant.   Is it not strange, Canidius,   20
That from Tarentum and Brundusium
He could so quickly cut the Ionian sea,
And take in Toryne ?   You have heard on 't, sweet ?

Cle. Celerity is never more admir'd
Than by the negligent.

Ant.   A good rebuke,
Which might have well become the best of men,
To taunt at slackness.   Canidius, we
Will fight with him by sea.

Cle.   By sea : what else ?

Can. Why will my lord do so ?

Ant.   For that he dares us to 't.

Eno. So hath my lord dar'd him to single fight.   30

Can. Ay, and to wage this battle at Pharsalia,
Where Cæsar fought with Pompey : but these offers,
Which serve not for his vantage, he shakes off,
And so should you.

Eno.   Your ships are not well mann'd,

Your mariners are muleters, reapers, people
Ingross'd by swift impress ; in Cæsar's fleet
Are those that often have 'gainst Pompey fought,
Their ships are yare, yours heavy : no disgrace
Shall fall you for refusing him at sea,
Being prepar'd for land.

Ant.   By sea, by sea.   40

Eno. Most worthy sir, you therein throw away
The absolute soldiership you have by land,
Distract your army, which doth most consist
Of war-mark'd footmen, leave unexecuted
Your own renowned knowledge, quite forgo
The way which promises assurance, and
Give up yourself merely to chance and hazard
From firm security.

Ant.   I 'll fight at sea.

Cle. I have sixty sails, Cæsar none better.

Ant. Our overplus of shipping will we burn ;   50
And, with the rest full-mann'd, from the head of
        Actium
Beat the approaching Cæsar.   But if we fail,
We then can do 't at land.

                    Enter a Messenger

                            Thy business ?

Mes. The news is true, my lord ; he is descried ;

Cæsar has taken Toryne.

Ant. Can he be there in person ? 'tis impossible ;
Strange, that his power should be.   Canidius,
Our nineteen legions thou shalt hold by land,
And our twelve thousand horse.   We 'll to our ship :
Away, my Thetis !

Enter a Soldier

How now, worthy soldier ?   60

Sol. O noble emperor, do not fight by sea,
Trust not to rotten planks.   Do you misdoubt
This   sword,   and   these   my   wounds ?   Let   the
Egyptians
And the Phœnicians go a-ducking : we
Have us'd to conquer, standing on the earth,
And fighting foot to foot.

Ant.   Well, well, away !

Exeunt Antony, Cleopatra, and Enobarbus

Sol. By Hercules, I think I am i' the right.

Can. Soldier, thou art : but his whole action grows
Not in the power on 't : so our leader 's led,
And we are women's men.

Sol.   You keep by land   70
The legions and the horse whole, do you not ?

Can. Marcus Octavius, Marcus Justeius,
Publicola and Cælius, are for sea :

But we keep whole by land.   This speed of Cæsar's
Carries beyond belief.

Sol.   While he was yet in Rome,
His power went out in such distractions as
Beguil'd all spies.

Can.   Who's his lieutenant, hear you?

Sol. They say, one Taurus.

Can.   Well I know the man.

Enter a Messenger

Mes. The emperor calls Canidius.

Can. With news the time's with labour, and throes forth   80
Each minute some.   *Exeunt*

SCENES VIII, IX, AND X

A plain near Actium

Enter Cæsar, and Taurus, with his army, marching

Cæs. Taurus!

Tau. My lord?

Cæs. Strike not by land, keep whole, provoke not battle
Till we have done at sea.   Do not exceed
The prescript of this scroll: our fortune lies
Upon this jump.   *Exeunt*

Enter Antony and Enobarbus

Ant. Set we our squadrons on yond side o' the hill,
In eye of Cæsar's battle, from which place
We may the number of the ships behold,
And so proceed accordingly.   *Exeunt*

Enter Canidius, marching with his land army one way over the stage; and Taurus, the lieutenant of Cæsar, with his army, the other way. After their going in, is heard the noise of a sea-fight.

Alarum. Enter Enobarbus

Eno. Naught, naught, all naught, I can behold no longer !
The Antoniad, the Egyptian admiral,
With all their sixty, fly and turn the rudder :
To see 't, mine eyes are blasted.

Enter Scarus

Sca.   Gods and goddesses,
All the whole synod of them !

Eno.   What 's thy passion ?

Sca. The greater cantle of the world is lost

With very ignorance, we have kiss'd away
Kingdoms and provinces.

Eno.   How appears the fight ?

Sca. On our side, like the token'd pestilence,
Where death is sure.   Yon ribaudred nag of Egypt   10
(Whom leprosy o'ertake !) i' the midst o' the fight,
When vantage like a pair of twins appear'd,
Both as the same, or rather ours the elder,
The breese upon her, like a cow in June,
Hoists sails and flies.

Eno. That I beheld :
Mine eyes did sicken at the sight, and could not
Endure a further view.

Sca.   She once being loof'd,   †
The noble ruin of her magic, Antony,
Claps on his sea-wing, and (like a doting mallard)   20
Leaving the fight in height, flies after her :
I never saw an action of such shame ;
Experience, manhood, honour, ne'er before
Did violate so itself.

Eno.   Alack, alack !

Enter Canidius

Can. Our fortune on the sea is out of breath,
And sinks most lamentably.   Had our general
Been what he knew himself, it had gone well :

O, he has given example for our flight
Most grossly by his own !

Eno. Ay, are you thereabouts ?   Why then good night   30
Indeed.

Can. Toward Peloponnesus are they fled.

Sca. 'Tis easy to 't ; and there I will attend
What further comes.

Can.   To Cæsar will I render
My legions and my horse : six kings already
Show me the way of yielding.

Eno.   I 'll yet follow
The wounded chance of Antony, though my reason
Sits in the wind against me.   *Exeunt*

SCENE XI

Alexandria.   Cleopatra's palace

Enter Antony with Attendants

Ant. Hark ! the land bids me tread no more upon 't,
It is asham'd to bear me.   Friends, come hither,
I am so lated in the world that I
Have lost my way for ever.   I have a ship
Laden with gold, take that, divide it ; fly,
And make your peace with Cæsar.

All.   Fly, not we.

Ant. I have fled myself, and have instructed cowards
     To run, and show their shoulders.   Friends, be gone ;
     I have myself resolv'd upon a course
     Which has no need of you ; be gone,   10
     My treasure 's in the harbour ; take it.   O,
     I follow'd that I blush to look upon,
     My very hairs do mutiny, for the white
     Reprove the brown for rashness, and they them
     For fear and doting.   Friends, be gone ; you shall
     Have letters from me to some friends that will
     Sweep your way for you.   Pray you, look not sad,
     Nor make replies of loathness, take the hint
     Which my despair proclaims ; let that be left
     Which leaves itself : to the sea-side straightway :   20
     I will possess you of that ship and treasure.
     Leave me, I pray, a little : pray you now,
     Nay, do so ; for indeed I have lost command,
     Therefore I pray you : I 'll see you by and by.

Sits down

Enter Cleopatra led by Charmian and Iras ;
Eros following

Er. Nay, gentle madam, to him, comfort him.

Ir. Do, most dear queen.

Cha. Do ! why, what else ?

91

Cle. Let me sit down.   O Juno !

Ant. No, no, no, no, no.

Er. See you here, sir ?   30

Ant. O fie, fie, fie !

Cha. Madam !

Ir. Madam, O good empress !

Er. Sir, sir !

Ant. Yes, my lord, yes ; he at Philippi kept
His sword e'en like a dancer, while I struck
The lean and wrinkled Cassius, and 'twas I
That the mad Brutus ended : he alone
Dealt on lieutenantry, and no practice had
In the brave squares of war : yet now—No matter.   40

Cle. Ah ! stand by.

Er. The queen, my lord, the queen.

Ir. Go to him, madam, speak to him,
He is unqualitied with very shame.

Cle. Well then, sustain me : O !

Er. Most noble sir, arise, the queen approaches,
Her head 's declin'd, and death will seize her, but
Your comfort makes the rescue.

Ant. I have offended reputation,
A most unnoble swerving.

Er.   Sir, the queen.   50

Ant. O, whither hast thou led me, Egypt ?   See,

    How I convey my shame out of thine eyes
    By looking back what I have left behind
    Stroy'd in dishonour.

Cle.   O my lord, my lord,
    Forgive my fearful sails !   I little thought
    You would have follow'd.

Ant.   Egypt, thou knew'st too well
    My heart was to thy rudder tied by the strings,
    And thou shouldst tow me after : o'er my spirit
    Thy full supremacy thou knew'st, and that
    Thy beck might from the bidding of the gods   60
    Command me

Cle.   O, my pardon !

Ant.   Now I must
    To the young man send humble treaties, dodge
    And palter in the shifts of lowness, who
    With half the bulk o' the world play'd as I pleas'd,
    Making and marring fortunes.   You did know
    How much you were my conqueror, and that
    My sword, made weak by my affection, would
    Obey it on all cause.

Cle.   Pardon, pardon !

Ant. Fall not a tear, I say, one of them rates
    All that is won and lost : give me a kiss,   70
    Even this repays me.   We sent our schoolmaster,   †

Is he come back ? Love, I am full of lead.
Some wine, within there, and our viands ! Fortune
    knows
We scorn her most, when most she offers blows.

Exeunt

SCENE XII

Egypt. Cæsar's camp

Enter Cæsar, Dolabella, Thyreus, with others

Cæs. Let him appear that's come from Antony.
    Know you him ?

Dol.   Cæsar, 'tis his schoolmaster,
    An argument that he is pluck'd, when hither
    He sends so poor a pinion of his wing,
    Which had superfluous kings for messengers,
    Not many moons gone by.

Enter Euphronius, ambassador from Antony

Cæs.   Approach, and speak.

Eu. Such as I am, I come from Antony :
    I was of late as petty to his ends
    As is the morn-dew on the myrtle-leaf
    To his grand sea.   †

Cæs.   Be't so : declare thine office.   10

Eu. Lord of his fortunes he salutes thee, and
Requires to live in Egypt, which not granted,
He lessens his requests, and to thee sues
To let him breathe between the heavens and earth,
A private man in Athens : this for him.
Next, Cleopatra does confess thy greatness,
Submits her to thy might, and of thee craves
The circle of the Ptolemies for her heirs,
Now hazarded to thy grace.

Cæs.   For Antony,
I have no ears to his request.   The queen   20
Of audience nor desire shall fail, so she
From Egypt drive her all-disgraced friend,
Or take his life there.   This if she perform,
She shall not sue unheard.   So to them both.

Eu. Fortune pursue thee !

Cæs.   Bring him through the bands.

                              Exit Euphronius

(*to Thyreus*) To try thy eloquence, now 'tis time,
        dispatch ;
From Antony win Cleopatra : promise,
And in our name, what she requires, add more,
From thine invention, offers : women are not
In their best fortunes strong ; but want will perjure   30
The ne'er-touch'd vestal : try thy cunning, Thyreus ;

  Make thine own edict for thy pains, which we
  Will answer as a law.

Thy.   Cæsar, I go.

Cæs. Observe how Antony becomes his flaw,
  And what thou think'st his very action speaks
  In every power that moves.

Thy.   Cæsar, I shall. *Exeunt*

SCENE XIII

Alexandria. Cleopatra's palace

Enter Cleopatra, Enobarbus, Charmian, and Iras

Cle. What shall we do, Enobarbus?

Eno.   Think, and die.

Cle. Is Antony or we in fault for this?

Eno. Antony only, that would make his will
  Lord of his reason. What though you fled
  From that great face of war, whose several ranges
  Frighted each other? Why should he follow?
  The itch of his affection should not then
  Have nick'd his captainship, at such a point,
  When half to half the world oppos'd, he being
  The mered question: 'twas a shame no less   10
  Than was his loss, to course your flying flags,

    And leave his navy gazing.

Cle.   .   Prithee, peace.

       Enter Antony, with Euphronius the Ambassador

Ant. Is that his answer ?

Eu. Ay, my lord.

Ant. The queen shall then have courtesy, so she
    Will yield us up.

Eu.   He says so.

Ant.   Let her know 't.
    To the boy Cæsar send this grizzled head,
    And he will fill thy wishes to the brim
    With principalities.

Cle.   That head, my lord ?

Ant. To him again, tell him he wears the rose   20
    Of youth upon him, from which the world should
        note
    Something particular : his coin, ships, legions,
    May be a coward's, whose ministers would prevail
    Under the service of a child as soon
    As i' the command of Cæsar : I dare him therefore
    To lay his gay comparisons apart
    And answer me declin'd, sword against sword,   †
    Ourselves alone.   I 'll write it : follow me.

                    Exeunt Antony and Euphronius

Eno. (*aside*) Yes, like enough ; high-battled Cæsar will

Unstate his happiness, and be stag'd to the show   30
Against a sworder !   I see men's judgements are
A parcel of their fortunes, and things outward
Do draw the inward quality after them,
To suffer all alike, that he should dream,
Knowing all measures, the full Cæsar will
Answer his emptiness ; Cæsar, thou hast subdu'd
His judgement too.

Enter a Servant

Ser.   A messenger from Cæsar.
Cle. What, no more ceremony ?   See, my women,
Against the blown rose may they stop their nose
That kneel'd unto the buds.   Admit him, sir.   40

Exit Servant

Eno. (*aside*) Mine honesty, and I, begin to square.
The loyalty well held to fools does make
Our faith mere folly : yet he that can endure
To follow with allegiance a fall'n lord
Does conquer him that did his master conquer,
And earns a place i' the story.

Enter Thyreus

Cle.   Cæsar's will !
Thy. Hear it apart.
Cle.   None but friends : say boldly.
Thy. So, haply, are they friends to Antony.

En. He needs as many, sir, as Cæsar has,
　　Or needs not us.   If Cæsar please, our master　　50
　　Will leap to be his friend : for us, you know,
　　Whose he is we are, and that is Cæsar's.

Thy.　　　　　　　　　　　　　　So.
　　Thus then, thou most renown'd, Cæsar entreats
　　Not to consider in what case thou stand'st
　　Further than he is Cæsar.

Cle.　　　　　　　　　　Go on : right royal.

Thy. He knows that you embrace not Antony
　　As you did love, but as you fear'd him.

Cle.　　　　　　　　　　　　　　O !

Thy. The scars upon your honour therefore he
　　Does pity, as constrained blemishes,
　　Not as deserv'd.

Cle.　　　　　　　He is a god and knows　　60
　　What is most right : mine honour was not yielded,
　　But conquer'd merely.

Eno.　　　　　　(*aside*) To be sure of that,
　　I will ask Antony.　Sir, sir, thou art so leaky
　　That we must leave thee to thy sinking, for
　　Thy dearest quit thee.　　　　　　　　*Exit*

Thy.　　　　　　　　Shall I say to Cæsar
　　What you require of him ? for he partly begs
　　To be desir'd to give.　It much would please him,

99

That of his fortunes you should make a staff
To lean upon : but it would warm his spirits,
To hear from me you had left Antony,   70
And put yourself under his shrowd,
The universal landlord.

Cle.   What 's your name ?

Thy. My name is Thyreus.

Cle.   Most kind messenger,
Say to great Cæsar this in deputation ;
I kiss his conquering hand : tell him, I am prompt
To lay my crown at 's feet, and there to kneel :
Tell him, from his all-obeying breath I hear
The doom of Egypt.

Thy.   'Tis your noblest course.
Wisdom and fortune combating together,
If that the former dare but what it can,   80
No chance may shake it.   Give me grace to lay
My duty on your hand.

Cle.   Your Cæsar's father oft,
(When he hath mus'd of taking kingdoms in)
Bestow'd his lips on that unworthy place,
As it rain'd kisses.

         Re-enter Antony and Enobarbus

Ant.   Favours ?   By Jove that thunders !—
What art thou, fellow ?

Thy.   One that but performs
          The bidding of the fullest man, and worthiest
          To have command obey'd.
Eno.   (*aside*) You will be whipp'd.
Ant. Approach, there !   Ah, you kite !   Now, gods and
               devils !
          Authority melts from me of late.   When I cried ' Ho ! '   90
          Like boys unto a muss, kings would start forth,
          And cry ' Your will ? '   Have you no ears ?
          I am Antony yet.

Enter Attendants

                    Take hence this Jack, and whip him.
Eno. (*aside*) 'Tis better playing with a lion's whelp,
          Than with an old one dying.
Ant.   Moon and stars,
          Whip him !   Were 't twenty of the greatest tributaries
          That do acknowledge Cæsar, should I find them
          So saucy with the hand of she here,—what 's her
               name,
          Since she was Cleopatra ?   Whip him, fellows,
          Till, like a boy, you see him cringe his face,   100
          And whine aloud for mercy.   Take him hence.
Thy. Mark Antony,—
Ant.   Tug him away : being whipp'd,
          Bring him again, the Jack of Cæsar's shall

Bear us an errand to him.

Exeunt Attendants, with Thyreus

You were half blasted ere I knew you : ha !
Have I my pillow left unpress'd in Rome,
Forborne the getting of a lawful race,
And by a gem of women, to be abus'd
By one that looks on feeders ?

Cle.   Good my lord,—

Ant. You have been a boggler ever,   110
But when we in our viciousness grow hard
(O misery on 't !) the wise gods seel our eyes ;
In our own filth drop our clear judgements, make us
Adore our errors, laugh at 's while we strut
To our confusion.

Cle.   O, is 't come to this ?

Ant. I found you as a morsel, cold upon
Dead Cæsar's trencher ; nay, you were a fragment
Of Cneius Pompey's, besides what hotter hours
Unregister'd in vulgar fame, you have
Luxuriously pick'd out : for I am sure,   120
Though you can guess what temperance should be,
You know not what it is.

Cle.   Wherefore is this ?

Ant. To let a fellow that will take rewards,
And say ' God quit you ! ' be familiar with

My playfellow, your hand ; this kingly seal
And plighter of high hearts !   O, that I were
Upon the hill of Basan, to outroar
The horned herd ! for I have savage cause,
And to proclaim it civilly, were like
A halter'd neck which does the hangman thank   130
For being yare about him.

Re-enter Attendants, with Thyreus

Is he whipp'd ?

1.*A.* Soundly, my lord.

Ant.   Cried he ? and begg'd a pardon ?

1.*A.* He did ask favour.

Ant. If that thy father live, let him repent
Thou wast not made his daughter, and be thou sorry
To follow Cæsar in his triumph, since
Thou hast been whipp'd for following him : hence-
       forth
The white hand of a lady fever thee,
Shake thou to look on 't.   Get thee back to Cæsar,
Tell him thy entertainment : look thou say   140
He makes me angry with him ; for he seems
Proud and disdainful, harping on what I am,
Not what he knew I was : he makes me angry,
And at this time most easy 'tis to do 't ;
When my good stars, that were my former guides,

103

Have empty left their orbs, and shot their fires
Into the abysm of hell.   If he mislike
My speech, and what is done, tell him he has
Hipparchus, my enfranched bondman, whom
He may at pleasure whip, or hang, or torture,　　　150
As he shall like to quit me : urge it thou :
Hence with thy stripes, begone !　　　*Exit Thyreus*

Cle. Have you done yet ?

Ant.　　　　　　　　Alack, our terrene moon
Is now eclips'd, and it portends alone
The fall of Antony.

Cle.　　　　　　　I must stay his time ?

Ant. To flatter Cæsar, would you mingle eyes
With one that ties his points ?

Cle.　　　　　　　　　Not know me yet ?

Ant. Cold-hearted toward me ?

Cle.　　　　　　　Ah, dear, if I be so,
From my cold heart let heaven engender hail,
And poison it in the source, and the first stone　　160
Drop in my neck : as it determines, so
Dissolve my life, the next Cæsarion smite,
Till by degrees the memory of my womb,
Together with my brave Egyptians all,
By the discandying of this pelleted storm
Lie graveless, till the flies and gnats of Nile

Have buried them for prey !

Ant.   I am satisfied.
Cæsar sits down in Alexandria, where
I will oppose his fate.   Our force by land
Hath nobly held, our sever'd navy too   170
Have knit again, and fleet, threatening most sea-like.
Where hast thou been, my heart ?   Dost thou hear,
        lady ?
If from the field I shall return once more
To kiss these lips, I will appear in blood,
I, and my sword, will earn our chronicle ;
There 's hope in 't yet.

Cle. That 's my brave lord !

Ant. I will be treble-sinew'd, hearted, breath'd,
And fight maliciously : for when mine hours
Were nice and lucky, men did ransom lives   †
Of me for jests ; but now I 'll set my teeth,   181
And send to darkness all that stop me.   Come,
Let 's have one other gaudy night : call to me
All my sad captains, fill our bowls once more :
Let 's mock the midnight bell.

Cle.   It is my birth-day,
I had thought to have held it poor, but since my lord
Is Antony again, I will be Cleopatra.

Ant. We will yet do well.

Cle. Call all his noble captains to my lord.

Ant. Do so, we'll speak to them, and to-night I'll force   190
    The wine peep through their scars.   Come on, my
      queen,
    There's sap in't yet.   The next time I do fight
    I'll make death love me ; for I will contend
    Even with his pestilent scythe.

                                 Exeunt all but Enobarbus

Eno. Now he'll outstare the lightning.   To be furious
    Is to be frighted out of fear, and in that mood
    The dove will peck the estridge ; and I see still,
    A diminution in our captain's brain
    Restores his heart : when valour preys on reason,
    It eats the sword it fights with.   I will seek   200
    Some way to leave him.   *Exit*

Act Fourth

SCENE I

Before Alexandria.   Cæsar's camp

Enter Cæsar, Agrippa, and Mæcenas, with his army :
Cæsar reading a letter

Cæs. He calls me boy, and chides as he had power
 To beat me out of Egypt ; my messenger
 He hath whipp'd with rods, dares me to personal
   combat :
 Cæsar to Antony ; let the old ruffian know
 I have many other ways to die ; meantime
 Laugh at his challenge.

Mæ.   Cæsar must think,
 When one so great begins to rage, he 's hunted
 Even to falling.   Give him no breath, but now
 Make boot of his distraction ; never anger
 Made good guard for itself.

Cæs.   Let our best heads   10
 Know that to-morrow the last of many battles
 We mean to fight.   Within our files there are,
 Of those that serv'd Mark Antony but late,

Enough to fetch him in.   See it done :
And feast the army ; we have store to do 't,
And they have earn'd the waste.   Poor Antony !

Exeunt

SCENE II

Alexandria.   Cleopatra's palace

Enter Antony, Cleopatra, Enobarbus, Charmian, Iras,
Alexas, with others

Ant. He will not fight with me, Domitius ?
Eno.   No.
Ant. Why should he not ?
Eno. He thinks, being twenty times of better fortune,
He is twenty men to one.
Ant.   To-morrow, soldier,
By sea and land I 'll fight : or I will live,
Or bathe my dying honour in the blood
Shall make it live again.   Woo 't thou fight well ?
Eno. I 'll strike, and cry ' Take all.'
Ant.   Well said, come on.
Call forth my household servants, let 's to-night
Be bounteous at our meal.

Enter three or four Servitors

Give me thy hand,   10

Thou hast been rightly honest ;—so hast thou ;—
Thou,—and thou,—and thou : you have serv'd me well,
And kings have been your fellows.

Cle.   (*aside to Eno.*) What means this ?

Eno. (*aside to Cle.*) 'Tis one of those odd tricks which
         sorrow shoots
Out of the mind.

Ant.   And thou art honest too :
I wish I could be made so many men,
And all of you clapp'd up together in
An Antony ; that I might do you service,
So good as you have done.

Ser.   The gods forbid !

Ant. Well, my good fellows, wait on me to-night :   20
Scant not my cups, and make as much of me
As when mine empire was your fellow too,
And suffer'd my command.

Cle.   (*aside to Eno.*) What does he mean ?

Eno. (*aside to Cle.*) To make his followers weep.

Ant.   Tend me to-night ;
May be it is the period of your duty,
Haply you shall not see me more, or if,
A mangled shadow : perchance to-morrow
You 'll serve another master.   I look on you,
As one that takes his leave.   Mine honest friends,

I turn you not away, but, like a master　　　　30
Married to your good service, stay till death :
Tend me to-night two hours, I ask no more,
And the gods yield you for 't !

Eno.　　　　　　　　　　What mean you, sir,
To give them this discomfort ?　Look, they weep,
And I, an ass, am onion-eyed : for shame,
Transform us not to women.

Ant.　　　　　　　　Ho, ho, ho !
Now the witch take me, if I meant it thus !
Grace grow where those drops fall !　My hearty friends,
You take me in too dolorous a sense,
For I spake to you for your comfort, did desire you　40
To burn this night with torches : know, my hearts,
I hope well of to-morrow, and will lead you
Where rather I 'll expect victorious life,
Than death, and honour.　Let 's to supper, come,
And drown consideration.　　　　　　　*Exeunt*

SCENE III

The same.　Before the palace

Enter two Soldiers to their guard

1.*S.* Brother, good night : to-morrow is the day.
2.*S.* It will determine one way : fare you well.

Heard you of nothing strange about the streets ?

1.*S.* Nothing.   What news ?

2.*S.* Belike 'tis but a rumour ; good night to you.

1.*S.* Well, sir, good night.

Enter other Soldiers

2.*S.* Soldiers, have careful watch.

3.*S.* And you.   Good night, good night.

They place themselves in every corner of the stage

4.*S.* Here we : and if to-morrow
    Our navy thrive, I have an absolute hope   10
    Our landmen will stand up.

3.*S.*   'Tis a brave army,
    And full of purpose.

Music of the hautboys is under the stage

4.*S.*   Peace, what noise ?

1.*S.*   List, list !

2.*S.* Hark !

1.*S.*   Music i' the air.

3.*S.*   Under the earth.

4.*S.* It signs well, does it not ?

3.*S.*   No.

1.*S.*   Peace, I say !
    What should this mean ?

2.*S.* 'Tis the god Hercules, whom Antony lov'd,
    Now leaves him.

1.*S.* Walk, let 's see if other watchmen
 Do hear what we do.

2.*S.* How now, masters !   20

All. (*speaking together*) How now ? How now ? Do you
 hear this ?

1.*S.* Ay, is 't not strange ?

3.*S.* Do you hear, masters ? do you hear ?

1.*S.* Follow the noise so far as we have quarter ;
 Let 's see how it will give off.

All. Content. 'Tis strange.   *Exeunt*

SCENE IV

The same. A room in the palace

Enter Antony and Cleopatra, Charmian and others attending

Ant. Eros ! mine armour, Eros !

Cle.   Sleep a little.

Ant. No, my chuck, Eros, come, mine armour, Eros !

     Enter Eros with armour

 Come, good fellow, put thine iron on :
 If fortune be not ours to-day, it is
 Because we brave her : come.

Cle.   Nay, I 'll help too.

What 's this for ?

Ant.   Ah, let be, let be ! thou art
The armourer of my heart : false, false ; this, this.

Cle. Sooth, la, I 'll help : thus it must be.

Ant.   Well, well,
We shall thrive now.   Seest thou, my good fellow ?
Go put on thy defences.

Er.   Briefly, sir.   10

Cle. Is not this buckled well ?

Ant.   Rarely, rarely :
He that unbuckles this, till we do please
To daff 't for our repose, shall hear a storm.
Thou fumblest, Eros, and my queen 's a squire
More tight at this than thou : dispatch.   O love,
That thou couldst see my wars to-day, and knew'st
The royal occupation ! thou shouldst see
A workman in 't.

                    Enter an armed Soldier

                    Good morrow to thee ; welcome :
Thou look'st like him that knows a warlike charge :
To business that we love we rise betime,   20
And go to 't with delight.

Sol. A thousand, sir, early though 't be, have on
Their riveted trim, and at the port expect you.

                         Shout.   Trumpets flourish

Enter Captains and Soldiers

Cap. The morn is fair.   Good morrow, general.

All. Good morrow, general.

Ant.   'Tis well blown, lads :
This morning, like the spirit of a youth
That means to be of note, begins betimes.
So, so ; come, give me that : this way ; well said.
Fare thee well, dame, whate'er becomes of me,
This is a soldier's kiss : rebukeable   30
And worthy shameful check it were, to stand
On more mechanic compliment ; I 'll leave thee
Now like a man of steel.   You that will fight,
Follow me close, I 'll bring you to 't.   Adieu.

   Exeunt Antony, Eros, Captains, and Soldiers

Cha. Please you retire to your chamber ?

Cle.   Lead me.
He goes forth gallantly.   That he and Cæsar might
Determine this great war in single fight !
Then Antony—but now—Well, on.   *Exeunt*

SCENE V

Alexandria.   Antony's camp

*Trumpets sound.   Enter Antony and Eros ; a Soldier
meeting them*

Sol. The gods make this a happy day to Antony !

Ant. Would thou, and those thy scars, had once prevail'd
To make me fight at land !

Sol.   Hadst thou done so,
The kings that have revolted, and the soldier
That has this morning left thee, would have still
Follow'd thy heels.

Ant.   Who 's gone this morning ?

Sol.   Who ?
One ever near thee : call for Enobarbus,
He shall not hear thee, or from Cæsar's camp
Say ' I am none of thine.'

Ant.   What say'st thou ?

Sol.   Sir,
He is with Cæsar.

Er.   Sir, his chests and treasure   10
He has not with him.

Ant.   Is he gone ?

Sol.   Most certain.

Ant. Go, Eros, send his treasure after, do it,
    Detain no jot, I charge thee : write to him
    (I will subscribe) gentle adieus, and greetings ;
    Say, that I wish he never find more cause
    To change a master.   O, my fortunes have
    Corrupted honest men ! Dispatch. Enobarbus !

                                Exeunt

SCENE VI

Alexandria.   Cæsar's camp

*Flourish.   Enter Cæsar with Agrippa, Enobarbus,
and others*

Cæs. Go forth, Agrippa, and begin the fight :
    Our will is Antony be took alive ;
    Make it so known.

Agr. Cæsar, I shall.   *Exit*

Cæs. The time of universal peace is near :
    Prove this a prosperous day, the three-nook'd world †
    Shall bear the olive freely.

                Enter a Messenger

Mes.   Antony
    Is come into the field.

Cæs.   Go charge Agrippa,

Plant those that have revolted in the van,
That Antony may seem to spend his fury   10
Upon himself.   *Exeunt all but Enobarbus*
Eno. Alexas did revolt, and went to Jewry
On affairs of Antony, there did dissuade
Great Herod to incline himself to Cæsar,
And leave his master Antony : for this pains,
Cæsar hath hang'd him.   Canidius and the rest
That fell away have entertainment, but
No honourable trust.   I have done ill,
Of which I do accuse myself so sorely
That I will joy no more.
                    Enter a Soldier of Cæsar's
Sol.   Enobarbus, Antony   20
Hath after thee sent all thy treasure, with
His bounty overplus : the messenger
Came on my guard, and at thy tent is now
Unloading of his mules.
Eno.   I give it you.
Sol. Mock not, Enobarbus,
I tell you true : best you saf'd the bringer   †
Out of the host ; I must attend mine office,
Or would have done 't myself.   Your emperor
Continues still a Jove.   *Exit*
Eno. I am alone the villain of the earth,   30

117

And feel I am so most.   O Antony,
Thou mine of bounty, how would'st thou have paid
My better service, when my turpitude
Thou dost so crown with gold !   This blows my heart :
If swift thought break it not, a swifter mean
Shall outstrike thought : but thought will do 't, I feel.
I fight against thee ?   No : I will go seek
Some ditch, wherein to die ; the foul'st best fits
My latter part of life.   *Exit*

SCENE VII

Field of battle between the camps

Alarum. Drums and trumpets. Enter Agrippa and others

Agr. Retire, we have engag'd ourselves too far :
Cæsar himself has work, and our oppression
Exceeds what we expected.   *Exeunt*
       Alarums.   Enter Antony, and Scarus wounded
Sca. O my brave emperor, this is fought indeed !
Had we done so at first, we had droven them home
With clouts about their heads.
Ant.   Thou bleed'st apace.
Sca. I had a wound here that was like a T,
But now 'tis made an H.   *Retreat afar off*

Ant.   They do retire.

Sca. We 'll beat 'em into bench-holes, I have yet

Room for six scotches more.   10

Enter Eros

Er. They are beaten, sir, and our advantage serves

For a fair victory.

Scar.   Let us score their backs,

And snatch 'em up, as we take hares, behind :

'Tis sport to maul a runner.

Ant.   I will reward thee

Once for thy spritely comfort, and ten-fold

For thy good valour. Come thee on.

Sca.   I 'll halt after. *Exeunt*

SCENE VIII

Under the walls of Alexandria

Alarum.   Enter Antony, in a march ; Scarus, with others

Ant. We have beat him to his camp : run one before,

And let the queen know of our gests. To-morrow,

Before the sun shall see 's, we 'll spill the blood

That has to-day escap'd. I thank you all ;

For doughty-handed are you, and have fought

Not as you serv'd the cause, but as 't had been

Each man's like mine; you have shown all Hectors.
Enter the city, clip your wives, your friends,
Tell them your feats, whilst they with joyful tears
Wash the congealment from your wounds and kiss   10
The honour'd gashes whole.   *(to Scarus)* Give me
      thy hand;

                    Enter Cleopatra, attended

To this great fairy I'll commend thy acts,
Make her thanks bless thee.   O thou day o' the
      world,
Chain mine arm'd neck, leap thou, attire and all,
Through proof of harness to my heart, and there
Ride on the pants triumphing!

Cle.   Lord of lords!
O infinite virtue, com'st thou smiling from
The world's great snare uncaught?

Ant.   My nightingale,
We have beat them to their beds.   What, girl!
      though grey
Do something mingle with our younger brown, yet
      ha' we   20
A brain that nourishes our nerves, and can
Get goal for goal of youth.   Behold this man,
Commend unto his lips thy favouring hand:
Kiss it, my warrior: he hath fought to-day

As if a god in hate of mankind had
Destroy'd in such a shape.

Cle.   I'll give thee, friend,
An armour all of gold ; it was a king's.

Ant. He has deserv'd it, were it carbuncled
Like holy Phœbus' car.   Give me thy hand,
Through Alexandria make a jolly march,   30
Bear our hack'd targets like the men that owe them :
Had our great palace the capacity
To camp this host, we all would sup together,
And drink carouses to the next day's fate,
Which promises royal peril.   Trumpeters,
With brazen din blast you the city's ear,
Make mingle with our rattling tabourines,
That heaven and earth may strike their sounds
      together,
Applauding our approach.   *Exeunt*

SCENE IX

Cæsar's camp

Enter sentinels

1.*S.* If we be not reliev'd within this hour,
We must return to the court of guard : the night

    Is shiny, and they say we shall embattle
    By the second hour i' the morn.

2.S.   This last day was
    A shrewd one to 's.

                      Enter Enobarbus

Eno.   O, bear me witness, night,—

3.S. What man is this ?

2.S.   Stand close, and list him.

Eno. Be witness to me, O thou blessed moon,
    When men revolted shall upon record
    Bear hateful memory, poor Enobarbus did
    Before thy face repent !

1.S.   Enobarbus !

3.S.   Peace !   10
    Hark further.

Eno. O sovereign mistress of true melancholy,
    The poisonous damp of night disponge upon me,
    That life, a very rebel to my will,
    May hang no longer on me : throw my heart
    Against the flint and hardness of my fault,
    Which, being dried with grief, will break to powder,
    And finish all foul thoughts.   O Antony,
    Nobler than my revolt is infamous,
    Forgive me in thine own particular,   20
    But let the world rank me in register

A master-leaver and a fugitive :
O Antony !   O Antony !   *Dies*

2.*S.*   Let's speak to him.

1.*S.* Let's hear him, for the things he speaks
May concern Cæsar.

3.*S.*   Let's do so.   But he sleeps.

1.*S.* Swoons rather, for so bad a prayer as his
Was never yet for sleep.

2.*S.*   Go we to him.

3.*S.* Awake, sir, awake, speak to us.

2.*S.*   Hear you, sir ?

1.*S.* The hand of death hath raught him.   (*Drums afar
off.*)   Hark ! the drums
Demurely wake the sleepers.   Let us bear him   30
To the court of guard ; he is of note : our hour
Is fully out.

3.*S.* Come on, then ; he may recover yet.

                              Exeunt with the body

SCENES X, XI, AND XII

Between the two camps

Enter Antony and Scarus, with their army

Ant. Their preparation is to-day by sea,
We please them not by land.

123

Sca.   · For both, my lord.

Ant. I would they 'ld fight i' the fire, or i' the air ;
     We 'ld fight there too.   But this it is ; our foot
     Upon the hills adjoining to the city
     Shall stay with us : order for sea is given ;
     They have put forth the haven . . .
     Where their appointment we may best discover
     And look on their endeavour.   *Exeunt*

Enter Cæsar, and his Army

Cæs. But being charg'd, we will be still by land,
     Which, as I take 't, we shall ; for his best force
     Is forth to man his galleys.   To the vales,
     And hold our best advantage.   *Exeunt*

Enter Antony and Scarus

Ant. Yet they are not join'd : where yond pine does stand,
     I shall discover all : I 'll bring thee word
     Straight, how 'tis like to go.   *Exit*
                       Alarum afar off, as at a sea-fight

Scar.   Swallows have built
In Cleopatra's sails their nests : the augurers
Say they know not, they cannot tell, look grimly,
And dare not speak their knowledge.   Antony
Is valiant, and dejected, and by starts
His fretted fortunes give him hope and fear
Of what he has, and has not.

Re-enter Antony

Ant.   All is lost ;
This foul Egyptian hath betrayed me :   10
My fleet hath yielded to the foe, and yonder
They cast their caps up, and carouse together
Like friends long lost.   Triple-turn'd whore, 'tis thou
Hast sold me to this novice, and my heart
Makes only wars on thee.   Bid them all fly ;
For when I am reveng'd upon my charm,
I have done all.   Bid them all fly ; begone.

Exit Scarus

O sun, thy uprise shall I see no more,
Fortune and Antony part here, even here
Do we shake hands.   All come to this ?   The hearts   20
That spaniel'd me at heels, to whom I gave
Their wishes, do discandy, melt their sweets
On blossoming Cæsar ; and this pine is bark'd,
That overtopp'd them all.   Betray'd I am.

125

O this false soul of Egypt! this grave charm,
Whose eye beck'd forth my wars, and call'd them home;
Whose bosom was my crownet, my chief end,
Like a right gipsy, hath at fast and loose   †
Beguil'd me, to the very heart of loss.
What, Eros, Eros!

                    Enter Cleopatra

                    Ah, thou spell!   Avaunt!   30
Cle. Why is my lord enrag'd against his love?
Ant. Vanish, or I shall give thee thy deserving,
And blemish Cæsar's triumph.   Let him take thee,
And hoist thee up to the shouting plebeians,
Follow his chariot, like the greatest spot
Of all thy sex.   Most monster-like be shown
For poor'st diminutives, for dolts; and let
Patient Octavia plough thy visage up
With her prepared nails.   *Exit Cleopatra*
                    'Tis well thou 'rt gone,
If it be well to live; but better 'twere   40
Thou fell'st into my fury, for one death
Might have prevented many.   Eros, ho!
The shirt of Nessus is upon me: teach me,   †
Alcides, thou mine ancestor, thy rage:
Let me lodge Lichas on the horns o' the moon,
And with those hands that grasp'd the heaviest club

Subdue my worthiest self.   The witch shall die :
To the young Roman boy she hath sold me, and I fall
Under this plot : she dies for 't.   Eros, ho !

Exit

SCENES XIII AND XIV

Alexandria.   Cleopatra's palace

Enter Cleopatra, Charmian, Iras, and Mardian

Cle. Help me, my women ! O, he is more mad
    Than Telamon for his shield ; the boar of Thessaly †
    Was never so emboss'd.

Cha.   To the monument,
    There lock yourself, and send him word you are dead.
    The soul and body rive not more in parting
    Than greatness going off.

Cle.   To the monument !
    Mardian, go tell him I have slain myself ;
    Say that the last I spoke was ' Antony,'
    And word it, prithee, piteously : hence, Mardian,
    And bring me how he takes my death.   To the
       monument !   *Exeunt* 10

Enter Antony and Eros

Ant. Eros, thou yet behold'st me?

Er.   Ay, noble lord.

Ant. Sometime we see a cloud that's dragonish,

A vapour sometime, like a bear, or lion,

A tower'd citadel, a pendent rock,

A forked mountain, or blue promontory

With trees upon't, that nod unto the world,

And mock our eyes with air: thou hast seen these signs,

They are black vesper's pageants.   †

Er.   Ay, my lord.

Ant. That which is now a horse, even with a thought

The rack dislimns, and makes it indistinct   10

As water is in water.

Er.   It does, my lord.

Ant. My good knave Eros, now thy captain is

Even such a body: here I am Antony,

Yet cannot hold this visible shape, my knave.

I made these wars for Egypt, and the queen,

Whose heart I thought I had, for she had mine,

(Which, whilst it was mine, had annex'd unto't

A million moe, now lost) she, Eros, has

Pack'd cards with Cæsar, and false-play'd my glory

Unto an enemy's triumph.   20
Nay, weep not, gentle Eros, there is left us
Ourselves to end ourselves.

Enter Mardian

                    O, thy vile lady !
She has robb'd me of my sword.

Mar.   No, Antony ;
My mistress lov'd thee, and her fortunes mingled
With thine entirely.

Ant.   Hence, saucy eunuch ; peace !
She hath betray'd me, and shall die the death.

Mar. Death of one person can be paid but once,
And that she has discharg'd : what thou wouldst do
Is done unto thy hand : the last she spake
Was ' Antony ! most noble Antony ! '   30
Then in the midst a tearing groan did break
The name of Antony ; it was divided
Between her heart and lips : she render'd life,
Thy name so buried in her.

Ant.   Dead then ?

Mar.   Dead.

Ant. Unarm, Eros, the long day's task is done,
And we must sleep. *(to Mar.)* That thou depart'st
    hence safe
Does pay thy labour richly ; go.   *Exit Mardian*

                         Off, pluck off,
The seven-fold shield of Ajax cannot keep
The battery from my heart.   O, cleave, my sides !
Heart, once be stronger than thy continent,   40
Crack thy frail case !   Apace, Eros, apace !
No more a soldier : bruised pieces, go,
You have been nobly borne.   From me awhile.

                              Exit Eros

I will o'ertake thee, Cleopatra, and
Weep for my pardon.   So it must be, for now
All length is torture : since the torch is out,
Lie down and stray no farther.   Now all labour
Mars what it does ; yea, very force entangles
Itself with strength : seal then, and all is done.
Eros !—I come, my queen.   Eros !—Stay for me :   50
Where souls do couch on flowers, we 'll hand in hand,
And with our sprightly port make the ghosts gaze :
Dido and her Æneas shall want troops,
And all the haunt be ours.   Come, Eros, Eros !

                       Re-enter Eros

Er. What would my lord ?
Ant.   Since Cleopatra died
I have liv'd in such dishonour, that the gods
Detest my baseness.   I, that with my sword
Quarter'd the world, and o'er green Neptune's back

With ships made cities, condemn myself to lack
The courage of a woman, less noble mind   60
Than she which by her death our Cæsar tells
' I am conqueror of myself.'   Thou art sworn, Eros,
That, when the exigent should come—which now
Is come indeed—when I should see behind me
The inevitable prosecution of
Disgrace and horror, that, on my command,
Thou then wouldst kill me : do 't ; the time is come :
Thou strikest not me, 'tis Cæsar thou defeat'st.
Put colour in thy cheek.

Er.   The gods withhold me !
Shall I do that which all the Parthian darts,   70
(Though enemy) lost aim and could not ?

Ant.   Eros,
Wouldst thou be window'd in great Rome, and see
Thy master thus with pleach'd arms, bending down
His corrigible neck, his face subdu'd
To penetrative shame, whilst the wheel'd seat
Of fortunate Cæsar, drawn before him, branded
His baseness that ensued ?

Er.   I would not see 't.

Ant. Come, then ; for with a wound I must be cur'd.
Draw that thy honest sword, which thou hast worn
Most useful for thy country.

Er.   O, sir, pardon me !   80

Ant. When I did make thee free, swor'st thou not then
     To do this when I bade thee ?   Do it at once,
     Or thy precedent services are all
     But accidents unpurpos'd.   Draw, and come.

Er. Turn from me then that noble countenance,
     Wherein the worship of the whole world lies.

Ant. Lo thee !   *Turning from him*

Er. My sword is drawn.

Ant.   Then let it do at once
     The thing why thou hast drawn it.

Er.   My dear master,
     My captain, and my emperor ; let me say,   90
     Before I strike this bloody stroke, farewell.

Ant. 'Tis said, man, and farewell.

Er. Farewell, great chief.   Shall I strike now ?

Ant.   Now, Eros.

Er. Why, there then : thus I do escape the sorrow
     Of Antony's death.   *Kills himself*

Ant.   Thrice-nobler than myself !
     Thou teachest me, O valiant Eros, what
     I should, and thou couldst not.   My queen and Eros
     Have by their brave instruction got upon me   †
     A nobleness in record : but I will be
     A bridegroom in my death, and run into 't   100

As to a lover's bed.   Come then, and, Eros,
Thy master dies thy scholar : to do thus

Falling on his sword

I learn'd of thee.   How ! not dead ? not dead ?
The guard, ho !   O, dispatch me !

Enter Dercetas and Guard

1.*G.*   What's the noise ?
Ant. I have done my work ill, friends : O, make an end
Of what I have begun.
2.*G.*   The star is fall'n.
1.*G.* And time is at his period.
All.   Alas, and woe !
Ant. Let him that loves me strike me dead.
1.*G.*   Not I.
2.*G.* Nor I.
3.*G.* Nor any one.   *Exeunt Guard* 110
Der. Thy death and fortunes bid thy followers fly.
This sword but shown to Cæsar, with this tidings,
Shall enter me with him.

Enter Diomedes

Dio. Where's Antony ?
Der.   There, Diomed, there.
Dio.   Lives he ?
Wilt thou not answer, man ?   *Exit Dercetas*

Ant. Art thou there, Diomed? Draw thy sword, and give me
    Sufficing strokes for death.

Dio.   Most absolute lord,
    My mistress Cleopatra sent me to thee.

Ant. When did she send thee?

Dio.   Now, my lord.

Ant.   Where is she

Dio. Lock'd in her monument. She had a prophesying fear   120
    Of what hath come to pass: for when she saw
    (Which never shall be found) you did suspect
    She had dispos'd with Cæsar, and that your rage
    Would not be purg'd, she sent you word she was dead;
    But, fearing since how it might work, hath sent
    Me to proclaim the truth; and I am come,
    I dread, too late.

Ant. Too late, good Diomed: call my guard, I prithee.

Dio. What, ho, the emperor's guard! The guard, what, ho!
    Come, your lords calls.   130

        Enter four or five of the Guard of Antony

Ant. Bear me, good friends, where Cleopatra bides;
    'Tis the last service that I shall command you.

1.G. Woe, woe are we, sir, you may not live to wear
    All your true followers out.

All.   Most heavy day !

Ant. Nay, good my fellows, do not please sharp fate
To grace it with your sorrows : bid that welcome
Which comes to punish us, and we punish it
Seeming to bear it lightly.   Take me up,
I have led you oft, carry me now, good friends,
And have my thanks for all.   *Exeunt, bearing Antony* 140

SCENE XV

The same.   A monument

*Enter Cleopatra, and her maids aloft, with Charmian,
and Iras*

Cle. O Charmian, I will never go from hence.

Cha. Be comforted, dear madam.

Cle.   No, I will not :
All strange and terrible events are welcome,
But comforts we despise ; our size of sorrow,
Proportion'd to our cause, must be as great
As that which makes it.

Enter, below, Diomedes

                    How now ? is he dead ?

Dio. His death's upon him, but not dead.
Look out o' the other side your monument ;

His guard have brought him thither.

Enter, below, Antony, borne by the Guard

Cle.   O sun,

Burn the great sphere thou mov'st in ! darkling stand   10
The varying shore o' the world.   O Antony,
Antony, Antony !   Help, Charmian, help, Iras, help ;
Help, friends below ; let 's draw him hither.

Ant.   Peace !

Not Cæsar's valour hath o'erthrown Antony,
But Antony's hath triumph'd on itself.

Cle. So it should be, that none but Antony
Should conquer Antony ; but woe 'tis so !

Ant. I am dying, Egypt, dying ; only
I here importune death awhile, until
Of many thousand kisses the poor last   20
I lay upon thy lips.

Cle.   I dare not, dear,

Dear my lord, pardon, I dare not,
Lest I be taken : not the imperious show
Of the full-fortun'd Cæsar ever shall
Be brooch'd with me, if knife, drugs, serpents, have
Edge, sting, or operation : I am safe :
Your wife Octavia, with her modest eyes,
And still conclusion, shall acquire no honour
Demuring upon me.   But come, come, Antony,—

136

Help me, my women,—we must draw thee up ;   30
Assist, good friends.

Ant.   O, quick, or I am gone.

Cle. Here's sport indeed !   How heavy weighs my lord !
Our strength is all gone into heaviness ;
That makes the weight.   Had I great Juno's power,
The strong-wing'd Mercury should fetch thee up,
And set thee by Jove's side.   Yet come a little—
Wishers were ever fools—O, come, come, come ;

They heave Antony aloft to Cleopatra

And welcome, welcome ! die where thou hast liv'd,
Quicken with kissing : had my lips that power,
Thus would I wear them out.

All.   A heavy sight !   40

Ant. I am dying, Egypt, dying :
Give me some wine, and let me speak a little.

Cle. No, let me speak, and let me rail so high,
That the false housewife Fortune break her wheel,
Provok'd by my offence.

Ant.   One word, sweet queen :
Of Cæsar seek your honour, with your safety.   O !

Cle. They do not go together.

Ant.   Gentle, hear me :
None about Cæsar trust but Proculeius.

Cle. My resolution, and my hands, I'll trust ;

137

<table>
<tr><td></td><td>None about Cæsar:</td><td>50</td></tr>
</table>

Ant. The miserable change now at my end
  Lament nor sorrow at ; but please your thoughts
  In feeding them with those my former fortunes
  Wherein I liv'd ; the greatest prince o' the world,
  The noblest ; and do now not basely die,
  Not cowardly put off my helmet to
  My countryman ; a Roman by a Roman
  Valiantly vanquish'd. Now my spirit is going,
  I can no more.

Cle.   Noblest of men, woo't die ?
  Hast thou no care of me ? shall I abide   60
  In this dull world, which in thy absence is
  No better than a sty ? O, see, my women,

              Antony dies

  The crown o' the earth doth melt. My lord ?
  O, wither'd is the garland of the war,
  The soldier's pole is fall'n : young boys and girls †
  Are level now with men ; the odds is gone,
  And there is nothing left remarkable
  Beneath the visiting moon.   *Faints*

Cha.   O, quietness, lady !
Iras. She 's dead, too, our sovereign.
Cha.   Lady !
Iras.   Madam !

Cha. O madam, madam, madam !
Iras.   Royal Egypt,   70
      Empress !
Cha.   Peace, peace, Iras !
Cle. No more but e'en a woman, and commanded
      By such poor passion as the maid that milks,
      And does the meanest chares.   It were for me
      To throw my sceptre at the injurious gods,
      To tell them that this world did equal theirs
      Till they had stol'n our jewel.   All 's but naught ;
      Patience is sottish, and impatience does
      Become a dog that 's mad : then is it sin
      To rush into the secret house of death,   80
      Ere death dare come to us ?   How do you, women ?
      What, what ? good cheer !   Why, how now, Charmian ?
      My noble girls ?   Ah, women, women ! look,
      Our lamp is spent, it 's out.   Good sirs, take heart,
      We 'll bury him ; and then, what 's brave, what 's
            noble,
      Let 's do it after the high Roman fashion,
      And make death proud to take us.   Come, away,
      This case of that huge spirit now is cold :
      Ah, women, women !   Come, we have no friend
      But resolution, and the briefest end.   90
            Exeunt : those above bearing off Antony's body

Act Fifth

SCENE I

Alexandria.   Cæsar's camp

*Enter Cæsar, Agrippa, Dolabella, Mæcenas, Gallus,
Proculeius, and others, his council of war*

Cæs. Go to him, Dolabella, bid him yield ;
Being so frustrate, tell him he mocks
The pauses that he makes.

Dol.   Cæsar, I shall.   *Exit*

Enter Dercetas, with the sword of Antony

Cæs. Wherefore is that ? and what art thou that dar'st
Appear thus to us ?

Der.   I am call'd Dercetas,
Mark Antony I serv'd, who best was worthy
Best to be serv'd : whilst he stood up and spoke,
He was my master, and I wore my life
To spend upon his haters.   If thou please
To take me to thee, as I was to him   10
I 'll be to Cæsar ; if thou pleasest not,
I yield thee up my life.

Cæs.   What is 't thou say'st ?

Der. I say, O Cæsar, Antony is dead.

Cæs. The breaking of so great a thing should make
    A greater crack : the round world
    Should have shook lions into civil streets,
    And citizens to their dens.   The death of Antony
    Is not a single doom ; in the name lay
    A moiety of the world.

Der.   He is dead, Cæsar,
    Not by a public minister of justice,   20
    Nor by a hired knife ; but that self hand,
    Which writ his honour in the acts it did,
    Hath, with the courage which the heart did lend it,
    Splitted the heart.   This is his sword,
    I robb'd his wound of it ; behold it stain'd
    With his most noble blood.

Cæs.   Look you sad, friends ?
    The gods rebuke me, but it is tidings
    To wash the eyes of kings.

Agr.   And strange it is
    That nature must compel us to lament
    Our most persisted deeds.

Mæ.   His taints and honours   30
    Wag'd equal with him.

Agr.   A rarer spirit never
    Did steer humanity : but you, gods, will give us

Some faults to make us men.   Cæsar is touch'd.

Mæ. When such a spacious mirror 's set before him,
He needs must see himself.

Cæs.   O Antony !
I have follow'd thee to this.   But we do lance
Diseases in our bodies : I must perforce
Have shown to thee such a declining day,
Or look'd on thine ; we could not stall together,
In the whole world : but yet let me lament,   40
With tears as sovereign as the blood of hearts,
Thou thou, my brother, my competitor
In top of all design ; my mate in empire,
Friend and companion in the front of war,
The arm of mine own body, and the heart
Where mine his thoughts did kindle ; that our stars
Unreconciliable should divide
Our equalness to this.   Hear me, good friends,—
                    Enter an Egyptian
But I will tell you at some meeter season,
The business of this man looks out of him,   50
We 'll hear him what he says.   Whence are you ?

Egy. A poor Egyptian yet ; the queen my mistress,
Confin'd in all she has, her monument,
Of thy intents desires instruction,
That she preparedly may frame herself

To the way she 's forc'd to.

Cæs.   Bid her have good heart,
She soon shall know of us, by some of ours,
How honourable and how kindly we
Determine for her ; for Cæsar cannot live
To be ungentle.

Egy.   So the gods preserve thee !   *Exit* 60

Cæs. Come hither, Proculeius.   Go and say,
We purpose her no shame : give her what comforts
The quality of her passion shall require ;
Lest in her greatness, by some mortal stroke,
She do defeat us ; for her life in Rome   †
Would be eternal in our triumph : go,
And with your speediest bring us what she says,
And how you find of her.

Pro.   Cæsar, I shall.   *Exit*

Cæs. Gallus, go you along. (*exit Gallus*.)   Where 's
        Dolabella,
To second Proculeius ?

All.   Dolabella !   70

Cæs. Let him alone, for I remember now
How he 's employ'd : he shall in time be ready.
Go with me to my tent, where you shall see
How hardly I was drawn into this war ;
How calm and gentle I proceeded still

      In all my writings : go with me, and see
      What I can show in this.   *Exeunt*

SCENE II

Alexandria.   The monument

Enter Cleopatra, Charmian, and Iras

Cle. My desolation does begin to make
      A better life.   'Tis paltry to be Cæsar ;
      Not being Fortune, he 's but Fortune's knave,
      A minister of her will : and it is great
      To do that thing that ends all other deeds,
      Which shackles accidents and bolts up change ;
      Which sleeps, and never palates more the dung,
      The beggar's nurse and Cæsar's.

*Enter, to the gates of the monument, Proculeius, Gallus,
              and Soldiers*

Pro. Cæsar sends greeting to the Queen of Egypt,
      And bids thee study on what fair demands   10
      Thou mean'st to have him grant thee.

Cle.   What 's thy name ?

Pro. My name is Proculeius.

Cle.   Antony

Did tell me of you, bade me trust you, but
I do not greatly care to be deceiv'd,
That have no use for trusting. If your master
Would have a queen his beggar, you must tell him,
That majesty, to keep decorum, must
No less beg than a kingdom : if he please
To give me conquer'd Egypt for my son,
He gives me so much of mine own as I   20
Will kneel to him with thanks.

Pro.   Be of good cheer ;
You 're fall'n into a princely hand, fear nothing,
Make your full reference freely to my lord,
Who is so full of grace that it flows over
On all that need.   Let me report to him
Your sweet dependency, and you shall find
A conqueror that will pray in aid for kindness,
Where he for grace is kneel'd to.

Cle.   Pray you, tell him
I am his fortune's vassal and I send him
The greatness he has got.   I hourly learn   30
A doctrine of obedience, and would gladly
Look him i' the face.

Pro.   This I 'll report, dear lady.
Have comfort, for I know your plight is pitied
Of him that caus'd it.

Gal. You see how easily she may be surpris'd.

> *Here Proculeius and two of the Guard ascend the monument by a ladder placed against a window, and, having descended, come behind Cleopatra. Some of the Guard unbar and open the gates*

Guard her till Cæsar come.   *Exit*

Iras. Royal queen !

Cha. O Cleopatra ! thou art taken, queen !

Cle. Quick, quick, good hands.   *Drawing a dagger*

Pro.   Hold, worthy lady, hold :
                                   Seizes and disarms her
Do not yourself such wrong, who are in this   40
Reliev'd, but not betray'd.

Cle.   What, of death too,
That rids our dogs of languish ?

Pro.   Cleopatra,
Do not abuse my master's bounty by
The undoing of yourself : let the world see
His nobleness well acted, which your death
Will never let come forth.

Cle.   Where art thou, death ?
Come hither, come ! come, come, and take a queen
Worth many babes and beggars !

Pro.   O, temperance, lady !

Cle. Sir, I will eat no meat, I 'll not drink, sir,

    If idle talk will once be necessary,   50
    I 'll not sleep neither : this mortal house I 'll ruin,
    Do Cæsar what he can.   Know, sir, that I
    Will not wait pinion'd at your master's court,
    Nor once be chastis'd with the sober eye
    Of dull Octavia.   Shall they hoist me up,
    And show me to the shouting varletry
    Of censuring Rome ?   Rather a ditch in Egypt
    Be gentle grave unto me, rather on Nilus' mud
    Lay me stark naked, and let the water-flies
    Blow me into abhorring ; rather make   60
    My country's high pyramides my gibbet,
    And hang me up in chains !

Pro.   You do extend
    These thoughts of horror further than you shall
    Find cause in Cæsar.

              Enter Dolabella

Dol.   Proculeius,
    What thou hast done thy master Cæsar knows,
    And he hath sent for thee : for the queen,
    I 'll take her to my guard.

Pro.   So, Dolabella,
    It shall content me best : be gentle to her.
    (*to Cle.*) To Cæsar I will speak what you shall please,
    If you 'll employ me to him.

Cle.   Say, I would die.   70

              Exeunt Proculeius and Soldiers

Dol. Most noble empress, you have heard of me ?

Cle. I cannot tell.

Dol.   Assuredly you know me.

Cle. No matter, sir, what I have heard or known.

    You laugh when boys or women tell their dreams ;

    Is 't not your trick ?

Dol.   I understand not, madam.

Cle. I dreamt there was an emperor Antony :

    O, such another sleep, that I might see

    But such another man !

Dol.   If it might please ye,—

Cle. His face was as the heavens, and therein stuck

    A sun and moon, which kept their course, and lighted

    The little O, the earth.

Dol.   Most sovereign creature,—   81

Cle. His legs bestrid the ocean, his rear'd arm

    Crested the world : his voice was propertied

    As all the tuned spheres, and that to friends ;

    But when he meant to quail, and shake the orb,

    He was as rattling thunder.   For his bounty,

    There was no winter in 't ; an autumn 'twas

    That grew the more by reaping : his delights

    Were dolphin-like, they show'd his back above

         The element they liv'd in : in his livery   90
         Walk'd crowns and crownets ; realms and islands were
         As plates dropp'd from his pocket.

Dol.   Cleopatra,—

Cle. Think you there was, or might be, such a man
        As this I dreamt of?

Dol.   Gentle madam, no.

Cle. You lie up to the hearing of the gods.
        But if there be, or ever were, one such,
        It 's past the size of dreaming : nature wants stuff
        To vie strange forms with fancy, yet to imagine
        An Antony, were nature's piece 'gainst fancy,
        Condemning shadows quite.

Dol.   Hear, me, good madam.   100
         Your loss is as yourself, great ; and you bear it
         As answering to the weight : would I might never
         O'ertake pursued success, but I do feel,
         By the rebound of yours, a grief that smites
         My very heart at root.

Cle.   I thank you, sir.
        Know you what Cæsar means to do with me ?

Dol. I am loath to tell you what I would you knew.

Cle. Nay, pray you, sir,—

Dol.   Though he be honourable,—

Cle. He 'll lead me then in triumph ?

Dol. Madam, he will, I know 't. 110

> *Flourish and shout within :* 'Make way there : Cæsar !'
> *Enter Cæsar, Gallus, Proculeius, Mæcenas, Seleucus, and
> others of his Train*

Cæs. Which is the Queen of Egypt ?

Dol. It is the emperor, madam. *Cleopatra kneels*

Cæs. Arise, you shall not kneel :
I pray you, rise, rise, Egypt.

Cle. Sir, the gods
Will have it thus, my master and my lord
I must obey.

Cæs. Take to you no hard thoughts :
The record of what injuries you did us,
Though written in our flesh, we shall remember
As things but done by chance.

Cle. Sole sir o' the world, 120
I cannot project mine own cause so well
To make it clear, but do confess I have
Been laden with like frailties, which before
Have often sham'd our sex.

Cæs. Cleopatra, know,
We will extenuate rather than enforce :
If you apply yourself to our intents,
Which towards you are most gentle, you shall find
A benefit in this change ; but if you seek

To lay on me a cruelty, by taking
Antony's course, you shall bereave yourself   130
Of my good purposes, and put your children
To that destruction which I'll guard them from,
If thereon you rely.   I'll take my leave.

Cle. And may, through all the world : 'tis yours ; and we,
Your scutcheons and your signs of conquest, shall
Hang in what place you please.   Here, my good lord.

Cæs. You shall advise me in all for Cleopatra.

Cle. This is the brief of money, plate and jewels,
I am possess'd of : 'tis exactly valued,
Not petty things admitted.   Where's Seleucus ?   140

Sel. Here, madam.

Cle. This is my treasurer : let him speak, my lord,
Upon his peril, that I have reserv'd
To myself nothing.   Speak the truth, Seleucus.

Sel. Madam,
I had rather seal my lips, than to my peril
Speak that which is not.

Cle.   What have I kept back ?

Sel. Enough to purchase what you have made known.

Cæs. Nay, blush not, Cleopatra, I approve
Your wisdom in the deed.

Cle.   See, Cæsar !   O, behold,   150
How pomp is follow'd ! mine will now be yours,

And, should we shift estates, yours would be mine.
The ingratitude of this Seleucus does
Even make me wild.   O slave, of no more trust
Than love that 's hir'd !   What, goest thou back ? thou
    shalt
Go back, I warrant thee ; but I 'll catch thine eyes,
Though they had wings : slave, soulless villain, dog !
O rarely base !

Cæs.   Good queen, let us entreat you.

Cle. O Cæsar, what a wounding shame is this,
That thou vouchsafing here to visit me,   160
Doing the honour of thy lordliness
To one so meek, that mine own servant should
Parcel the sum of my disgraces by   †
Addition of his envy !   Say, good Cæsar,
That I some lady trifles have reserv'd,
Immoment toys, things of such dignity
As we greet modern friends withal, and say,
Some nobler token I have kept apart
For Livia and Octavia, to induce
Their mediation, must I be unfolded   170
With one that I have bred ?   The gods ! it smites me
Beneath the fall I have.   (*to Seleucus*) Prithee, go
    hence,
Or I shall show the cinders of my spirits

Through the ashes of my chance : wert thou a man,
Thou wouldst have mercy on me.

Cæs.   Forbear, Seleucus.

Exit Seleucus

Cle. Be it known, that we, the greatest, are mis-thought
For things that others do ; and when we fall,
We answer others' merits in our name,
Are therefore to be pitied.

Cæs.   Cleopatra,
Not what you have reserv'd, nor what acknowledg'd,
Put we i' the roll of conquest : still be 't yours,   181
Bestow it at your pleasure, and believe
Cæsar's no merchant, to make price with you
Of things that merchants sold.   Therefore be cheer'd,
Make not your thoughts your prisons : no, dear queen,
For we intend so to dispose you, as
Yourself shall give us counsel.   Feed, and sleep :
Our care and pity is so much upon you,
That we remain your friend, and so adieu.

Cle. My master, and my lord !

Cæs.   Not so.   Adieu.   190

Flourish.   Exeunt Cæsar and his train

Cle. He words me, girls, he words me, that I should not
Be noble to myself : but, hark thee, Charmian.

Whispers Charmian

Iras. Finish, good lady, the bright day is done,
And we are for the dark.

Cle.   Hie thee again,
I have spoke already, and it is provided,
Go put it to the haste.

Cha.   Madam, I will.

Re-enter Dolabella

Dol. Where is the queen?

Cha.   Behold, sir.   *Exit*

Cle.   Dolabella!

Dol. Madam, as thereto sworn by your command,
(Which my love makes religion to obey)
I tell you this: Cæsar through Syria   200
Intends his journey, and within three days,
You with your children will he send before:
Make your best use of this: I have perform'd
Your pleasure, and my promise.

Cle.   Dolabella,
I shall remain your debtor.

Dol.   I your servant.
Adieu, good queen, I must attend on Cæsar.

Cle. Farewell, and thanks.   *Exit Dolabella*
              Now, Iras, what think'st thou?
Thou, an Egyptian puppet, shalt be shown
In Rome as well as I: mechanic slaves

With greasy aprons, rules, and hammers, shall   210
Uplift us to the view : in their thick breaths,
Rank of gross diet, shall we be enclouded
And forc'd to drink their vapour.

Iras.   The gods forbid !

Cle. Nay, 'tis most certain, Iras : saucy lictors
Will catch at us like strumpets, and scald rhymers
Ballad us out o' tune : the quick comedians
Extemporally will stage us, and present
Our Alexandrian revels ; Antony
Shall be brought drunken forth, and I shall see
Some squeaking Cleopatra boy my greatness   220
I' the posture of a whore.

Iras.   O the good gods !

Cle. Nay, that's certain.

Iras. I'll never see't ; for I am sure my nails
Are stronger than mine eyes.

Cle.   Why, that's the way
To fool their preparation, and to conquer
Their most absurd intents.

                    Re-enter Charmian

                        Now, Charmian !
Show me, my women, like a queen : go fetch
My best attires : I am again for Cydnus,
To meet Mark Antony : sirrah Iras, go,

Now, noble Charmian, we 'll dispatch indeed,   230
And when thou hast done this chare I 'll give thee leave
To play till doomsday. Bring our crown and all.

                Exit Iras.   *A noise within*

Wherefore 's this noise ?

             Enter a Guardsman

Gua.   Here is a rural fellow,
That will not be denied your highness' presence :
He brings you figs.

Cle. Let him come in.   *Exit Guardsman*
            What poor an instrument
May do a noble deed ! he brings me liberty.
My resolution 's plac'd, and I have nothing
Of woman in me : now from head to foot
I am marble-constant ; now the fleeting moon   240
No planet is of mine.

    Re-enter Guardsman, with Clown bringing in a basket

Gua.   This is the man.

Cle. Avoid, and leave him.   *Exit Guardsman*
Hast thou the pretty worm of Nilus there,
That kills and pains not ?

Clo. Truly, I have him : but I would not be the party
that should desire you to touch him, for his biting
is immortal ; those that do die of it do seldom or
never recover.

Cle. Rememberest thou any that have died on 't ?

Clo. Very many, men and women too. I heard of one 250
    of them no longer than yesterday, a very honest
    woman, but something given to lie, as a woman
    should not do, but in the way of honesty, how she
    died of the biting of it, what pain she felt : truly,
    she makes a very good report o' the worm ; but he
    that will believe all that they say, shall never be
    saved by half that they do : but this is most fallible,
    the worm 's an odd worm.

Cle. Get thee hence, farewell.

Clo. I wish you all joy of the worm. 260

Setting down his basket

Cle. Farewell.

Clo. You must think this, look you, that the worm will
    do his kind.

Cle. Ay, ay, farewell.

Clo. Look you, the worm is not to be trusted but in the
    keeping of wise people ; for indeed there is no
    goodness in the worm.

Cle. Take thou no care, it shall be heeded.

Clo. Very good. Give it nothing, I pray you, for it is
    not worth the feeding. 270

Cle. Will it eat me ?

Clo. You must not think I am so simple but I know the

> devil himself will not eat a woman : I know that a
> woman is a dish for the gods, if the devil dress her
> not.   But, truly, these same whoreson devils do the
> gods great harm in their women ; for in every ten
> that they make, the devils mar five.

Cle. Well, get thee gone, farewell.

Clo. Yes, forsooth : I wish you joy o' the worm.   *Exit*
> *Re-enter Iras with a robe, crown, &c.*

Cle. Give me my robe, put on my crown, I have   280
Immortal longings in me.   Now no more
The juice of Egypt's grape shall moist lip :
Yare, yare, good Iras ; quick !   Methinks I hear
Antony call ; I see him rouse himself
To praise my noble act ; I hear him mock
The luck of Cæsar, which the gods give men
To excuse their after wrath.   Husband, I come :
Now to that name my courage prove my title !
I am fire, and air ; my other elements
I give to baser life.   So, have you done ?   290
Come then, and take the last warmth of my lips.
Farewell, kind Charmian, Iras, long farewell.
> *Kisses them.   Iras falls and dies*

Have I the aspic in my lips ?   Dost fall ?
If thou and nature can so gently part,
The stroke of death is as a lover's pinch,

Which hurts, and is desir'd.   Dost thou lie still ?
If thus thou vanishest, thou tell'st the world
It is not worth leave-taking.

Cha. Dissolve, thick cloud, and rain, that I may say
The gods themselves do weep !

Cle.   This proves me base : 300
If she first meet the curled Antony,
He 'll make demand of her, and spend that kiss
Which is my heaven to have.   Come, thou mortal
        wretch,

            To an asp, which she applies to her breast

With thy sharp teeth this knot intrinsicate
Of life at once untie ; poor venomous fool,
Be angry, and dispatch.   O, couldst thou speak,
That I might hear thee call great Cæsar ass,
Unpolicied !

Cha.   O eastern star !

Cle.   Peace, peace !
Dost thou not see my baby at my breast,
That sucks the nurse asleep ?

Cha.   O, break !   O, break ! 310

Cle. As sweet as balm, as soft as air, as gentle.
O Antony !   Nay, I will take thee too :

            Applying another asp to her arm

What should I stay—   *Dies*

Cha. In this vile world ?   So, fare thee well.
Now boast thee, death, in thy possession lies
A lass unparallel'd.   Downy windows, close ;
And golden Phœbus never be beheld
Of eyes again so royal !   Your crown 's awry ;
I 'll mend it, and then play.

Enter the Guard, rushing in

1.*G.* Where is the queen ?

Cha.   Speak softly, wake her not.   320

1.*G.* Cæsar hath sent—

Cha.   Too slow a messenger.

Applies an asp

O, come apace, dispatch : I partly feel thee.

1.*G.* Approach, ho !   All 's not well : Cæsar 's beguil'd.

2.*G.* There 's Dolabella sent from Cæsar ; call him.

1.*G.* What work is here, Charmian ?   Is this well done ?

Cha. It is well done, and fitting for a princess
Descended of so many royal kings.
Ah, soldier !   *Dies*

Re-enter Dolabella

Dol. How goes it here ?

2.*G.*   All dead.

Dol.   Cæsar, thy thoughts
Touch their effects in this : thyself art coming   330
To see perform'd the dreaded act which thou

160

So sought'st to hinder.

Within.   ' A way there, a way for Cæsar ! '
Re-enter Cæsar and his train

Dol. O sir, you are too sure an augurer ;
That you did fear is done.

Cæs.   Bravest at the last,
She levell'd at our purposes, and being royal
Took her own way.   The manner of their deaths ?
I do not see them bleed.

Dol.   Who was last with them ?

1.G. A simple countryman, that brought her figs :
This was his basket.

Cæs.   Poison'd then.

1.G.   O Cæsar,
This Charmian liv'd but now, she stood and spake : 340
I found her trimming up the diadem
On her dead mistress ; tremblingly she stood,
And on the sudden dropp'd.

Cæs.   O noble weakness !
If they had swallow'd poison, 'twould appear
By external swelling : but she looks like sleep,
As she would catch another Antony
In her strong toil of grace.

Dol.   Here, on her breast,
There is a vent of blood, and something blown :

   The like is on her arm.

1.*G.* This is an aspic's trail, and these fig-leaves   350
   Have slime upon them, such as the aspic leaves
   Upon the caves of Nile.   †

Cæs.   Most probable
   That so she died ; for her physician tells me
   She hath pursued conclusions infinite
   Of easy ways to die. Take up her bed,
   And bear her women from the monument :
   She shall be buried by her Antony :
   No grave upon the earth shall clip in it
   A pair so famous. High events as these
   Strike those that make them ; and their story is 360
   No less in pity than his glory which
   Brought them to be lamented. Our army shall
   In solemn show attend this funeral,
   And then to Rome. Come, Dolabella, see
   High order in this great solemnity.   *Exeun.*

Notes

I. ii. (S.D.). The stage-direction is given as in F, but nothing else is heard of either Rannius or Lucilius.

I. ii. 4. *change*; so F. We should perhaps read *charge* (the usual and easy enough emendation).

I. ii. 27. *Herod of Jewry may do homage*; probably with no reference to the narrative of the gospels (in spite of ' that I may come and worship him also '), but simply as the type of blustering tyrant; cf. *Merry Wives of Windsor*, II. i. 20, '*What a Herod of Jewry is this !*'

I. ii. 32. *better than figs*; usually explained as ' a proverbial expression,' which it may well be, but no authority is adduced for the explanation. On the other hand, there is surely intended an ironic forecast of the basket of figs in Act V.

I. ii. 101. *Extended Asia*; . . . the line is normal, in spite of appearances, *Asia* being a trisyllable, and *Euphrates* (as usual at the time) short in the second.

I. ii. 195. *courser's hair*; it was an old belief that a horse hair laid in water would become an eel. (Cf. Colcroft, *Shakespeare Notes and Lectures*, where he explains the origin of the belief.)

I. iii. 37. *race of heaven*; either ' of divine descent ' or ' with a " tang " of the divine in it.'

I. iv. 78. *Both what by sea . . .*; as it stands this naturally means ' what (section of the enemy) I can at the moment confront '; but the meaning natural to the situation and to Shakespearean idiom would be ' with what force I can confront the present crisis.'

I. v. 47. *arm-gaunt*; there has been an infinity of explanation and emendation; but the word may stand as it is, in the sense of gaunt with bearing arms (though this particular seems little relevant here) and emendation is perilous.

II. ii. 43. *their contestation Was theme for you*; this has, very naturally, puzzled all the commentators, and various transpositions and more vigorous emendations have been suggested. All that one can be sure of is the intended sense, that the contestation in some way involved Antony so that he could be supposed to have 'practised' against Cæsar, a sense given rather clumsily, but perhaps rightly, by Malone's adaptation of Warburton's emendation, *Was them'd from you.*

II. ii. 53. *As matter whole you have (not) to make it with*; I have accepted with hesitation Rowe's drastic insertion of *not*, since F, though it gives perfectly good sense ('if you patch up a quarrel out of oddments, though you have sound enough grounds for one, it must not be with this particular oddment') does not seem to give the required sense.

II. ii. 134. *truth would be . . . truth*; i.e., whereas in the present state of instability rumours have the force of truth, in the serenity which the marriage would cause even true ill news would be reckoned idle tales.

II. ii. 176. *You stay'd well by 't*; the commentators are silent. But it does not appear in the least clear what this means. Perhaps either 'you did well' or 'you stuck to it well.'

II. ii. 207. *tended her . . . adornings*; the first part of the phrase presents little difficulty ('waited on her, while she watched them'), but a deal of ingenuity and erudition has been squandered on the second part. There seems no sort of reason for going beyond the straightforward meaning, accepted by the straightforward Steevens and Warburton, namely, that the gentlewomen as they moved gracefully (one might say even sinuously, as befitting mermaids) made a lovely frame for the lovelier picture.

II. iv. 6. *at Mount*; so F. Perhaps *at the Mount*, but I fancy that even at the cost of a hypermetric line we should read *at Mount Misenum*.

II. v. 103. *That art not what thou'rt sure of*; this phrase is as good an example as may be of a type of passage frequent in Shakespeare, more particularly in his later work, of which the meaning has to be, as it were, ' felt ' in a quick reading, rather than analytically understood. Cleopatra ' means ' ' it is the news of which you are so sure that deserves my anger, and not you, the bringer of it '; but all attempts to reword such passages do nothing but darken counsel. A great poet can express himself in his own poetic idiom and cannot be re-expressed in someone else's prose.

II. vii. 96. *Strike the vessels*; various suggestions; ' broach the casks,' ' clink the glasses together,' and, an attractive one by Case, ' fill the glasses to the brim,' with a transference of meaning from the sense of *strike* ' to smooth off the corn in a measure level with the brim.'

II. vii. 124. *Splits what it speaks*; an unhappily fissile combination of sounds!

II. vii. 134. *Hoo! says a'*; is *says a'* perhaps an auditory error for ' *sessa* ' ? (cf. *Lear*, III. iv. 101).

III. ii. 6. *the green sickness*; this is usually interpreted as a scornful attribution to Lepidus of a malady traditionally appropriated to love-lorn damsels; and this no doubt suits the lines which follow, but it is hard not to feel also (or instead) an allusion to Lepidus' poor head for drinking.

III. v. 16. *rush*; why in a garden should he spurn a rush in particular? Is it possible that this is not so appropriate to Antony in the garden as to Eros' illustrative action, kicking the rushes on the floor of the apartment.

III. vii. 5, 6. *If not denounc'd . . . person*; so Malone. F reads, *If not, denounc'd.* Much trouble; the natural meaning is ' if it is not expressly forbidden me, why may I not . . .' (Malone-Deighton), but the difficulty here is the common conjunction of ' denounce ' with ' war ' in the sense of ' declare ': another explanation is ' *even* if the war had not been declared against me (as it has) why should I not . . .' (Case), but the difficulty here is the need to supply the ' even.' Or we may take *denounce* as meaning simply ' explain,' and retain the F comma; but then *against* for *to* is awkward.

III. vii. 7–9. Again an odd silence of commentators. There is presumably a pun on two senses of *bear* and possibly another on two senses of *serve*; but I do not pretend that this throws much light.

III. x. 18. *loof'd*; (F actually reads *looft*). This is a common enough form of ' luff,' to bring a ship's head up into the wind. But it is odd that Shakespeare should use not only a technicality but a technicality which without further explanation is meaningless, since whether luffing is a preparation for flight or for closer action depends on where the wind is. And in any case the picture both here and in the corresponding passage in Plutarch is of Cleopatra's ships having their sails furled for the engagement and then hoisting them for flight. The word ought to mean either ' with sails set ' or ' in flight.'

III. xi. 71. *schoolmaster*; i.e. the tutor of his and Cleopatra's children.

III. xii. 9. *his grand sea*; there has been dispute about this, and some commentators have proposed *this* for *his*. But is there any difficulty in taking the phrase as meaning 'to the grand sea, which is what Antony is in comparison with me'?

III. xiii. 27. *And answer me declin'd, sword against sword*; it is tempting to emend to a characteristic Shakespearean rhythm, *And answer me, declined sword 'gainst sword.*

III. xiii. 180. *nice*; there has been some trouble about this, but I can see no reason to desert the usual Shakespearean meaning of *nice*, i.e. 'fastidious,' 'picking and choosing.' It is surely only a characteristically compressed way of saying, 'when in my days of good fortune I could pick and choose whom I spared or slew.'

IV. vi. 6. *three-nook'd world*; either as divided between the triumvirs, or the 'triplex mundus' (sea, earth, and sky), or (see Du Bartas) east, south, and west, ''twixt Sem and Cham and Japheth.'

IV. vi. 26. *true : best*; it looks as though *'twere* had dropped out before *best* through confusion with *true*.

IV. xii. 28. *fast and loose*; a 'cheating game,' thus described: 'A leathern belt is made up into a number of intricate folds, and placed edgewise upon a table. One of the folds is made to resemble the middle of the girdle, so that whoever should thrust a skewer into it would think he held it fast to the table; whereas, when he has so done, the person with whom he plays may take hold of both ends and draw it away.'

IV. xii. 43. *The shirt of Nessus*, etc.; Hercules shot the Centaur Nessus with a poisoned arrow; Nessus gave Hercules' wife his blood-stained (and therefore poisoned) shirt, telling her to give it to her husband if ever she needed to recapture his love. Later she gave it to Hercules, who in his death agony hurled his servant Lichas into the sea.

IV. xiii. 2. *Telamon for his shield*; Telamon was the 'surname' of Ajax, who when Odysseus and not himself was awarded the armour of the dead Achilles, went mad and killed himself.

the boar of Thessaly; sent by Artemis, in punishment for neglect, to ravage Calydon.

IV. xiv. 8. *pageants*; not just 'shows'; a pageant was an erection on wheels which could be drawn in a 'carnival' procession, like the disguised cars with their freight in a modern 'battle of flowers' or the Lord Mayor's show; the word is therefore exactly appropriate to the appearances of which Antony is talking.

IV. xiv. 98. *Have by their brave instruction* . . .; explanations are: 'Have, as my tutors in courage, won for themselves (upon me) a noble place in story' (Case) or 'forestalled me in gaining' (Rolfe). Neither seems easy to extract from the words of the text, or to give any particular force to the 'but' which follows. I feel that the phrase should mean 'have put before me a noble example to copy,' the emphasis lying on what they have done for Antony, not what glory they have won for themselves. But I am not sure that the words can bear that meaning. The words which follow I take to mean that Antony is not going to be a reluctant pupil but an ardent lover.

IV. xv. 65. *the soldier's pole*; this is commonly, and perhaps rightly, taken to mean the 'standard'; and in the preceding line *garland* can no doubt mean just 'glory'; but Deighton is surely right in seeing in the juxtaposition of the two words at least an allusion to the Maypole.

V. i. 65. *her life . . . triumph*; not 'her continuing to live in Rome,' but 'her presence, living, at my triumph in Rome would make it supreme' (or, if we are to press the sense of *eternal*, which may be no more than a vague superlative) 'make it eternally memorable.'

V. ii. 163. *Parcel*; this normally means 'divide up into smaller parts,' and it is possible to take the phrase to mean 'add one final item to my injuries'; but one feels that in fact Cleopatra means 'fill up the sum of my injuries.'

V. ii. 352. *caves*; ? *canes* (Barry).

Glossary

MANY words and phrases in Shakespeare require glossing, not because they are in themselves unfamiliar, but for the opposite reason, that Shakespeare uses in their Elizabethan and unfamiliar sense a large number of words which seem so familiar that there is no incentive to look for them in the glossary. It is hoped that a glossary arranged as below will make it easy to see at a glance what words and phrases in any particular scene require elucidation. A number of phrases are glossed by what seems to be, in their context, the modern equivalent rather than by lexicographical glosses on the words which compose them.

Act First

SCENE I

line
4 PLATED, mailed
6 FRONT (forehead, *and so*) face
8 RENEGES, renounces
  TEMPER, restraint
12 TRIPLE PILLAR OF THE WORLD, *i.e. the triumvir*
15 BEGGARY, beggarliness
16 BOURN, limit

line
18 GRATES ME, THE SUM, *i.e. 'the news chafes me—give me the summary'*
23 ENFRANCHISE, set free
28 PROCESS, command
34 RANG'D, ordered
39 WEET, know
46 STRETCH, extend
58 PROPERTY, quality
60 APPROVES, confirms

SCENE II

4 HORNS, the symbol of cuckoldry
61 CANNOT GO, is sterile
101 EXTENDED, seized
106 MINCE, soften
  TONGUE, report

112 EARING, ploughing (*i.e. to eradicate weeds*)
126 BY REVOLUTION LOWERING, diminishing by change
128 COULD, would be ready to

Act I Sc. ii—*continued*

line		line	
129	ENCHANTING, putting a charm on	169	CUT, grief
144	METTLE, ardour	180	EXPEDIENCE, haste
157	DISCREDITED YOUR TRAVEL, 'proved you a bad sight-seer'	184	CONTRIVING, working for us
		193	GOING ON, increasing
165	IT SHOWS . . . TAILORS, *i.e. the gods are like tailors*	194	DANGER, endanger

SCENE III

32	COLOUR, excuse	67	ARE, stand fast
33	STAYING, to stay	71	AFFECT, choose
36	BENT, expression, *or* arch		LACE, *i.e. of stays*
	SO POOR, however poor	81	MEETLY, well enough
48	SCRUPULOUS, hesitant	85	THE CARRIAGE OF HIS CHAFE, his furious bearing
54	MORE PARTICULAR, own affair		
55	SAFE, make secure	96	BECOMINGS, graces
61	GARBOILS, disturbances	97	EYE, appear

SCENE IV

3	COMPETITOR, partner	33	REBEL TO JUDGEMENT, are rebels against good sense
9	ABSTRACT, epitome		
19	THE TURN OF TIPPLING, drink for drink	39	DISCONTENTS, discontented men
		40	GIVE HIM, make him out
20	STAND THE BUFFET, exchange blows	41	PRIMAL STATE, creation
		49	EAR, plough
22	COMPOSURE, composition	52	FLUSH, vigorous
24	SOILS, blemishes	63	DID DEIGN, did not disdain
31	RATE, chide	71	LANK'D, grew thin

SCENE V

line
- 4 MANDRAGORA, mandrake (as opiate)
- 11 UNSEMINAR'D, castrated
- 24 BURGONET, helmet
- 29 BROAD-FRONTED, broad-browed

line
- 44 PIECE, amplify
- 49 BEASTLY DUMB'D, *either* silenced by a beast, *or* made silent as a beast
- 60 POSTS, messengers

Act Second

SCENE I

- 10 CRESCENT, growing (*with suggestion of moon picked up in 'to the full'*)
- 21 SALT, lustful
  WANN'D, paled
- 23 FIELD OF FEASTS, field of rich pasture (*from which the animal would not stray*)
- 26 PROROGUE, put off consideration of
- 45 PREGNANT, probable
  SQUARE, quarrel
- 50 IT ONLY . . . UPON, our one vital concern is

SCENE II

- 9 STOMACHING, resentment
- 25 CURSTNESS, bad temper
- 39 PRACTISE, plot against
- 40 MY QUESTION, right for me to inquire into
- 52 PATCH, vamp up
- 61 FRONTED, opposed
- 67 GARBOILS, disturbances
- 74 MISSIVE, messenger
- 80 BE . . . STRIFE, be no cause of quarrel
- 89 THE WHICH YOU BOTH, both of which you
- 102 ATONE, reconcile
- 133 IMPORT, betoken
- 138 PRESENT, impromptu
- 159 PRESENTLY, immediately
- 163 FAME, rumour
- 184 SQUARE, fair
- 204 GLOW, make to glow
- 211 YARELY FRAME THE OFFICE, perform the task neatly

Act II Sc. ii—continued

line
216 BUT FOR VACANCY, HAD GONE, but for leaving a vacuum, would have gone
225 ORDINARY, reckoning

line
228 CROPP'D, produced a crop
240 RIGGISH, wanton
243 BLESSED LOTTERY, lucky chance

SCENE III

6 KEPT MY SQUARE, stayed true (*met. from carpentry*)
18 DEMON, spirit
26 THICKENS, grows dim

36 ALL TO NOUGHT, any odds
37 INHOOP'D, enclosed (*so that they could not avoid fighting*)

SCENE V

1 MOODY, melancholy
10 ANGLE, fishing-tackle
22 TIRES, robes
23 PHILIPPAN, *the name of the sword* (*not an adj.*)
38 TART A FAVOUR, sour face
41 FORMAL, normal
50 ALLAY, water down
51 PRECEDENCE, what has preceded

58 TURN, purpose
71 BOOT, reward
96 NARCISSUS, a beautiful boy of Greek mythology
113 INCLINATION, disposition
116 GORGON, *i.e.* the particular Gorgon, Medusa, whose face turned men to stone

SCENE VI

10 FACTORS, agents
13 GHOSTED, appeared as ghost to
24 FEAR, frighten
26 O'ERCOUNT, outnumber
27 O'ERCOUNT, cheat
30 FROM THE PRESENT, irrelevant to the present discussion
33 EMBRAC'D, if you embrace it
34 TO TRY, if you try

47 AM WELL STUDIED, have thought long on my debt
58 COMPOSITION, agreement
73 TOWARD, in prospect
78 ENJOY, give rein to, 'indulge'
83 KNOWN, been acquainted
114 MADE, counted
119 CONVERSATION, behaviour

SCENE VII

<table>
<tr><td>line</td><td></td><td>line</td><td></td></tr>
<tr><td>5</td><td>ALMS-DRINK, dregs</td><td>68</td><td>INCLIPS, embraces</td></tr>
<tr><td>6</td><td>AS . . . DISPOSITION, (?) their dispositions grate on one another</td><td>92</td><td>ON WHEELS, i.e. fast</td></tr>
<tr><td></td><td></td><td>101</td><td>FROM ALL, from all food</td></tr>
<tr><td>13</td><td>PARTISAN, two-edged pike</td><td>109</td><td>BATTERY TO, assault on</td></tr>
<tr><td></td><td>SENNET, flourish of trumpets</td><td>111</td><td>HOLDING, burden</td></tr>
<tr><td>20</td><td>FOISON, plenty</td><td>114</td><td>EYNE, eyes</td></tr>
<tr><td>30</td><td>I'LL NE'ER OUT, I will not stand out</td><td>115</td><td>FATS, vats</td></tr>
<tr><td></td><td></td><td>120</td><td>OFF, to leave</td></tr>
<tr><td>31</td><td>IN, in drink</td><td>124</td><td>DISGUISE, drunkenness</td></tr>
<tr><td>42</td><td>IT, its</td><td>125</td><td>ANTICK'D, make fools of</td></tr>
<tr><td>50</td><td>EPICURE, fastidious gourmet</td><td>126</td><td>TRY, try conclusions with you</td></tr>
<tr><td>68</td><td>PALES, encloses</td><td>134</td><td>THERE'S MY CAP, i.e. he throws it up</td></tr>
</table>

Act Third

SCENE I

<table>
<tr><td>1</td><td>DARTING, arrow-shooting</td><td>34</td><td>JADED, driven jaded</td></tr>
<tr><td>17</td><td>IN THEIR OFFICER, by their subordinates</td><td></td><td></td></tr>
</table>

SCENE II

<table>
<tr><td>12</td><td>ARABIAN BIRD, the phœnix</td><td>51</td><td>CLOUD, dark mark</td></tr>
<tr><td>19</td><td>SHARDS (wing-cases, and so) wings</td><td>57</td><td>RHEUM, cold in head</td></tr>
<tr><td></td><td></td><td>58</td><td>CONFOUND, destroy</td></tr>
<tr><td>26</td><td>AS MY . . . APPROOF, as I would enter into a bond that you will prove</td><td></td><td></td></tr>
</table>

SCENE III

<table>
<tr><td>19</td><td>MOTION, moving</td><td>19</td><td>STATION, standing still</td></tr>
</table>

ANTONY AND CLEOPATRA

SCENE IV

3 SEMBLABLE, similar
6 SCANTLY, disparagingly
8 VENTED, uttered
10 FROM HIS TEETH, *i.e.* not from the heart

line
12 STOMACH, resent
24 BRANCHLESS, maimed
27 STAIN, overshadow

SCENE V

7 RIVALITY, equality
10 HIS OWN APPEAL, his (Cæsar's) own impeachment

11 UP, shut up
12 CHAPS, jaws

SCENE VI

20 QUEASY, 'sick of'
25 RATED, allotted
52 OSTENTATION, demonstration
61 OBSTRUCT, obstacle
80 WRONG LED, deluded

81 NEGLIGENT DANGER, *either* danger owing to negligence, *or* danger which we neglected
95 TRULL, harlot

SCENE VII

8 MERELY, utterly
13 TRADUC'D, blamed
18 FOR, as
23 TAKE IN, capture
36 INGROSS'D, assembled

36 IMPRESS, press-gang
38 YARE, handy
60 THETIS, sea-goddess
76 DISTRACTIONS, small detachments

SCENE VIII

5 PRESCRIPT, limits prescribed by | 6 JUMP, throw

SCENE IX

line
2 IN EYE, in sight

line
2 BATTLE, army

SCENE X

5 SYNOD, assembly
6 CANTLE, piece
9 TOKEN'D PESTILENCE, the plague with its 'tokens' or external symptoms

10 RIBAUDRED NAG, wanton jade
14 BREESE, gad-fly
20 MALLARD, wild-drake.

SCENE XI

3 LATED, benighted
39 DEALT ON LIEUTENANTRY, 'sat at headquarters'
40 SQUARES OF WAR, battle formation
44 UNQUALITIED, unmanned

54 STROY'D, destroyed
55 FEARFUL, terrified
60 BECK, beckoning
   FROM, contrary to
63 LOWNESS, humility

SCENE XII

5 SUPERFLUOUS, 'and to spare'
18 CIRCLE, crown
25 BANDS, army

33 ANSWER, obey, implement
34 BECOMES HIS FLAW, behaves in disaster

SCENE XIII

5 RANGES, lines (of the fleet)
8 NICK'D, cheated, *or* maimed
10 MERED, sole
11 COURSE, follow
22 PARTICULAR, outstanding
30 UNSTATE, divest himself of

41 SQUARE, quarrel
71 SHROUD, shelter
74 IN DEPUTATION, as my mouthpiece
83 TAKING IN, receiving submission of

Act III   Sc. xiii—*continued*

line
91 MUSS, scramble, 'scrum'
93 JACK, fellow
109 FEEDERS, servants
110 A BOGGLER, shifty
112 SEEL, close (*prop.* sew up eyes of hawk)
120 LUXURIOUSLY, lustfully
127 HILL OF BASAN, *cf.* 'bulls of Bashan' (*Psalms xxii and lxviii*)
128 HORNED, cuckolded
131 YARE, workmanlike

line
153 TERRENE, earthly
157 TIES HIS POINTS, is his valet (ties hose to doublet)
161 DETERMINES, ends
165 DISCANDYING, melting
171 FLEET, float
175 CHRONICLE, record
183 GAUDY, of festive commemoration
194 PESTILENT, deadly
197 ESTRIDGE, falcon

Act Fourth

SCENE I

9 MAKE BOOT, take advantage of

SCENE II

8 TAKE ALL, 'All or nothing'
14 SHOOTS OUT, produces from

25 PERIOD, end

SCENE III

10 ABSOLUTE, sure
   HAUTBOYS, oboes
14 SIGNS, augurs

24 AS . . . QUARTER, as our 'beat' extends
25 GIVE OFF, (?) cease

SCENE IV

line
11 RARELY, excellently
13 DAFF, put off
15 TIGHT, adroit

line
23 TRIM, equipment
31 CHECK, reprehension
32 MECHANIC, (?) elaborate

SCENE V

14 SUBSCRIBE, sign

SCENE VI

13 DISSUADE, persuade (*from his loyalty to Antony*)
18 HONOURABLE TRUST, position of trust

26 SAF'D, gave safe-conduct to
34 BLOWS, strikes

SCENE VII

2 HAS WORK, is hard put to it
6 CLOUTS, bandages
9 BENCH-HOLES, holes of privies

10 SCOTCHES, wounds
15 SPRITELY, spirited

SCENE VIII

2 GESTS, acts
8 CLIP, embrace
22 GET GOAL FOR GOAL OF, play level with

28 CARBUNCLED, bejewelled
31 TARGETS, shields
OWE, own
37 TABOURINES, drums

SCENE IX

2 COURT OF GUARD, guard-room
3 EMBATTLE, stand to arms
5 SHREWD, severe
6 LIST, listen to
9 BEAR HATEFUL MEMORY, be remembered with hatred

17 WHICH, *i.e.* the heart
20 IN THINE OWN PARTICULAR, *i.e.* yourself
28 RAUGHT, snatched
30 DEMURELY, with their subdued sound

SCENE XI

line
1 BUT BEING CHARG'D, unless we are attacked

line
1 STILL, quiet

SCENE XII

8 FRETTED, chequered
16 CHARM, enchantress
21 SPANIEL'D, followed dog-like
22 DISCANDY, melt
23 BARK'D stripped

25 GRAVE, deadly *or* potent, *or perhaps with modern sense*
27 CROWNET, coronet
28 RIGHT, true
37 FOR, to
DIMINUTIVES, weaklings

SCENE XIII

3 EMBOSS'D, foaming with rage
MONUMENT, the mausoleum (*which she had built for herself*)

5 RIVE, are painfully sundered

SCENE XIV

10 RACK DISLIMNS, the cloud-drift erases
12 KNAVE, squire
18 MOE, more (*Eliz. plural*)
19 PACK'D CARDS, cheated
39 BATTERY, stroke
40 CONTINENT, what contains
46 LENGTH, *sc. of time*
49 SEAL, conclude

52 PORT, bearing
58 QUARTER'D, divided
63 EXIGENT, need
65 PROSECUTION, pursuit
72 WINDOW'D, in a window
73 PLEACH'D, folded
74 CORRIGIBLE, submitting to correction

SCENE XV

line

10 DARKLING, in darkness
25 BROOCH'D, adorned
29 DEMURING, looking demurely
39 QUICKEN, gain life

line

74 CHARES, tasks
78 SOTTISH, stupid
79 BECOME, suits

Act Fifth

SCENE I

2 FRUSTRATE, baffled

HE MOCKS, ... MAKES, the delays he tries to make are folly

19 MOIETY, half (*Lepidus not being reckoned*)

31 WAG'D EQUAL, were equally balanced (*as in an 'evens' bet*)

39 STALL TOGETHER, be 'stable-mates'
41 SOVEREIGN, heartfelt
42 COMPETITOR, associate
63 PASSION, emotion
74 HARDLY, 'against the grain'

SCENE II

16 BEGGAR, suppliant

83 CRESTED, overtopped like a crest (*a not uncommon crest was a raised arm*)

WAS PROPERTIED, had the quality of

85 QUAIL, frighten
92 PLATES, silver coins
121 PROJECT, set out
140 ADMITTED, included
166 IMMOMENT, trivial
167 MODERN, common
183 MAKE PRIZE, make a valuation
214 LICTORS, consul's officers

215 SCALD, petty
220 BOY, *because the Eliz. actors of women's parts were boys*
226 ABSURD, outrageous
231 CHARE, task
263 KIND, nature
283 YARE, quick!
301 CURLED, curly-haired
304 INTRINSICATE, intricate
308 UNPOLICIED, frustrated
335 LEVELL'D (aimed, *and so*) guessed
348 VENT, ooze
358 CLIP, embrace